VOICES OF TYRANNY

TEMPLES OF SILENCE

VOICES OF TYRANNY

TEMPLES OF SILENCE

R. MURRAY SCHAFER

ARCANA
EDITIONS

Published by Arcana Editions, Indian River, Ontario, KOL 2BO, Canada.

ISBN 1-895127-17-3 (cloth)
ISBN 1-895127-19-X (paper)

Manuscript preparation by Jean Elliott.
Edited by Jean Donelson.
Designed by William Rueter.
Cover illustration by the author.
Second printing at Commercial Press, Peterborough, Ontario.

CONTENTS

Preface 7

1 **Ursound** 11

2 **Acoustic Space** 29

3 **Three Documentary Studies** 45

> The Dialectical Soundscape 45
> The Closed Soundscape 52
> The Open Soundscape 57

4 **Three Reflections** 63

> The Deceptive Soundscape 63
> The Glazed Soundscape 67
> The Crowded Soundscape 73

5 **The Canadian Soundscape** 83

6 **The Soundscape Designer** 101

7 **Music and the Soundscape** 115

8 **Radical Radio** 131

9 **Musecology** 145

10 **I Have Never Seen a Sound** 161

PREFACE

'No,' said the salesman spontaneously from the midst of his wall of books. As the supervisor of the self-help section he was surrounded by hundreds of subjects. 'No.' Then slightly more accommodatingly, 'What's it called?'

'*The Tuning of the World*,' I repeated, 'by R. Murray Schafer, S-C-H ... I think it's out of print now but I thought ...'

'Music section.'

'But it's not about music,' I protested, 'it's about sounds, quite ordinary, everyday sounds.'

'Ah,' said the salesman, 'Esoterica.'   (*Form*, IV, 1991)

When *The Tuning of the World* was first published in 1977, booksellers said it opened up such a new subject that they could find no appropriate place for it on their shelves. Had I been consulted, I might have suggested they leave it in the display window. I was passionately devoted to the idea that by making the public aware of the soundscape, noise pollution would soon be vanquished and we would be propelled in the direction of intelligent acoustic design. The book had been well received by experts in a great variety of disciplines: architecture, urbanology, geography, acoustical engineering, music, communications and environmental studies. This I found encouraging, without realizing that it only contributed to the booksellers' dilemma, and I can imagine many dialogues similar to that reprinted above from a recent German magazine. While *The Tuning of the World* went into several languages, it quickly disappeared from the stores. To keep it available in my own country, I bought back the Canadian edition. It marked the beginning of a new era, for since that time I have published all my own work through Arcana Editions, a cottage industry run from my own home. Of course things don't circulate as widely today as formerly, but they are more effectively available for those who really want them. Now, fifteen years after *The Tuning of the World,* I am bringing out the present volume, perhaps smaller in scope than the first book, but no less hopefully written, for the soundscape has not sufficiently improved, and the problem of excessive noise in our lives remains. *The Tuning of the World* was a digest of research conducted by the World Soundscape Project at Simon Fraser University, Vancouver, between 1970 and 1975. Since that time this work has been extended by other researchers, notably in Japan, France and Northern Europe.

In 1975 I left Vancouver to live on a farm in Ontario. Failing the facilities for active research, my own work on the soundscape has taken the form of teaching and reflecting, and it is these activities that have generated the present collection of essays over the years since 1977. This is one of two books I am publishing simultaneously. The other, *A Sound Education,* consists of one hundred listening and soundmaking exercises and is clearly intended for classroom use with the hope of sensitizing a generation of young people to environmental sounds and encouraging them to consider ways of designing future soundscapes. The present book consists of essays written for a variety of publications, some academic and some more popular. Included also is lecture material from a soundscape course I gave a few years ago at McGill University. This accounts for the change of tone from chapter to chapter. I have left this since I don't think it is particularly important for this book to form a unity or *Gradus ad Parnassum* of soundscape studies. It is a series of utterances, like sounds themselves, each occurring at its own point in time or space, some carefully prepared, others more spontaneous or passionately argued. To have arranged things in a more linear progression, to have given them a methodology, would have been to surrender to the visually dominant culture and its love of systems that stands in opposition to the uncontrollable world of sounds. I will have more to say about this in the closing essay, 'I Have Never Seen a Sound.'

Soundscape researchers have frequently been accused of lacking methodology or a coherent plan, as if the final goal was to be some huge design embracing all the sounds of the world in an acoustic New World Order. But since all sounds exist in the present tense, any such attempt would be quite impossible. All one can do is to alert more people to the present state of affairs with the hope that whatever the future brings, it may be less discordant than the present. Noise is often a commodity, manufactured and sold with a purpose. Whether it is a siren, a motorcycle or a radio makes little difference; behind every item is an institution seeking profit from dissonance. These are the Voices of Tyranny. Against them are ranked the Temples of Silence, the quiet environments where sounds are more conspicuous by their scarcity. There is exuberance here but there is no waste. We think of a temple, but it is really an attitude of mind, and it is one we need to recover in the modern world.

The rhythms and communication systems of the natural soundscape teach us that God was, or is, among other things, a first-rate acoustical engineer. There are simply no sounds in nature that will destroy your hearing. I have often thought of this as I listen to the interactive messages of the natural soundscape, where there is always a time for sounding and a time for listening. Even when I move my limbs I marvel at how quietly they move and wonder what sound they would have made if they had been designed in the factories of the Industrial Revolution or the assembly lines of Detroit. Think of how carefully the human ear was created, sensitive enough to hear the minutest whisper but not so sensitive as to pick up the crashing together of air molecules or the blood coursing through our bodies. Supposing the ear had been placed next to the mouth where it would have picked up the feedback of smacking lips and clattering teeth. As for Detroit's accomplishment, the most I can say of the automobile is that the sound it resembles most is the fart. As if in anthropomorphic irony, the exhaust system is even positioned where the anus would be, though quite without the sphincter muscles for controlling emissions in public assembly.

That is why I find myself returning repeatedly to nature for clues as to what soundscape design might become if we paid more attention to the 'great open secret' of nature and less to the circuses of civilization. Some critics found *The Tuning of the World* regressive for this reason, accusing me of unrealistic sentimentality. But notions of forwards or backwards belong only to societies addicted to progress, just as poverty is a notion that springs from a rage for wealth. I don't believe in progress in the sense that increased wealth or technology is, in itself, redemptive. As for going back, it can't be back if you've never been there; and there is, after all, a very satisfying musical form known as ternary in which the original material returns with the significant difference that it follows a contrasting interlude.

So these essays explore soundscapes I've tried to inhabit, either personally or by examining documents from other places or times. The main concern is to try to discover clues that might be useful, so that, as future soundscapes evolve, they might, in a limited way at least, be rendered more satisfying and conducive to the better life we all hope lies ahead.

Indian River, Summer 1992

1 URSOUND

Ursound, the first sound, the original creative force. To comprehend its power as creator and shaper we go back to cosmogonic myths. Such myths attempt to explain how the world relates to the cosmos and how man came to be centered in the world. The mystery is dark, the myths vary, employing symbols for clarification. Aside from their importance for religious dogma, creation myths can also be interpreted as attempts to describe the gradual clarification of consciousness. As such they give clues to how the faculties of perception originated, or at least clues to how they functioned in relationship to each other among the divine and human figures whose activities constitute the most ancient reference point we can study.

In Genesis we learn how 'the spirit of God' (which we may conceive as breath, pneuma or wind) moved over the 'darkness ... of the deep' (a metaphor for the unconscious). If the text is read attentively, it is clear that the first stroke was not the distinction between darkness and light, but rather the acoustic announcement of intention: 'And God said ...' We imagine these words, emphatically repeated, as a series of mighty vibrations, cleaving the universe into form. Each act of shaping is prefaced by the same sound-symbol.[1] Only after each action does the visual mode of experiencing come into play: 'And God saw that it was good.'

Everything relates back to the collision of wind and water, the creative point where sound originated. We would like to press further into this mystery but it is impossible; the data are not precise; and in any case, as I showed in *The Tuning of the World*, the acoustic sym-

---

1 '... "symbol" being taken to mean the best possible expression for a complex fact not yet clearly apprehended by consciousness.' C.G. Jung, *Collected Works*, vol. 8, p.75.

The gods forge creatively with a 'sacred' noise. Source: *Historia de Gentibus Septentrio-Nalibus*, Olaus Magnus, Basel, 1567.

bolism of wind and water is complex and never easy to explain. The relationship between God and the dark waters that prefigured creation is also unclear, so much so that the Audians and Sampsaeans, early heretical sects, believed that God did not create the waters, since nowhere in Genesis do we read: 'And God said, let there be waters.' St. Augustine attacked this idea in *The City of God*, reaffirming the orthodox belief that God, being All, was both the waters and the breath of air that rushed over them. Certainly the Bible is clear in telling us that the sound hypostasized in the meeting of these two elements was the voice of God. Is it possible that the 'darkness of the deep' is not only a metaphor for the chronicler's ignorance but also for God's unconsciousness of his own powers? Then God also appears to participate in the development from blind instinct to cognition as man's appreciation of God's refinement grows.[2]

For the ancient Semites the 'vault' or 'firmament' described in Genesis 1:6 was a solid dome, holding the upper waters of heaven in check. Thus the infinitude of the unconscious had both an upper and a lower realm, between which rested the discernible elements that formed the subtle and ever-widening realm of consciousness. The range of conscious distinctions opens out quickly in the following verses: grasses and herbs appear, then trees, animals, fishes and finally man. Details are added to the original broad strokes, and soon a picture of the world is created that no one can have difficulty in recognizing. One searches the account for a range of acoustic discriminations to match the visual description and fails to find it: man's exclamation of pleasure at the creation of woman (2:23), the voice of the serpent (3:1) or of woman (3:2) are not comparably evocative to what our eyes may behold. But we would be mistaken to think that sound, having functioned so creatively at the opening of the myth, is so quickly relegated to secondary importance. In fact it continues to be the medium by which God and man communicate, and therefore maintains the position of primary importance throughout the Bible – but I shall come back to this after comparing some creation myths from other sources.

In the Egyptian creation myths the names of the gods sometimes vary, but one idea is carried through them all. Atum (sometimes Re)

2 Jung's essay *Answer to Job* is an excellent exposition of this dual development in discrimination.

initiated creation by climbing out of the abysmal waters (Nun) onto a primeval hill where he then brought the other gods into being. Atum (Re) says: 'I am the great god who came into being by himself.' But in other versions we read that it was Nun who first created himself. Again the ambivalence about whether water was the creative element or the element from which creation proceeded. But the differentiation of the primal substance only begins when Atum (Re) names the parts of his body; from this naming the other gods are born.

He is Re, who created the names of the parts of his body. That is how these gods who follow him came into being.[3]

When the First Dynasty established its capital at Memphis, the Memphite god Ptah was proclaimed the First Principle and thereby assumed the powers of Atum (Re). Ptah conceives the elements of the universe with his mind ('heart') and brings them into being by his speech ('tongue'). In the Egyptian myths the articulation of consciousness takes the form of naming things. There is an approach here to the Logos Doctrine, later amplified by the Greeks and taken up subsequently by the early Christians, as the fourth gospel shows. Logos (the Word) was then conceived as 'the Word of the Lord,' i.e., divine reason, the guiding principle of the universe. Whether the Greek Logos was ever to be understood as uttered sound or merely as a mental construct is a matter of dispute.[4] But there is no doubt about the relationship between thought and sound in the Memphite creation myth.

There came into being as the heart and there came into being as the tongue (something) in the form of Atum.[5]

3 'Egyptian Myths, Tales and Mortuary Texts,' in *Ancient and Near Eastern Texts Pertaining to the Old Testament*, ed. J.B. Pritchard, Third Edition (Princeton, N.J., 1969), p.4.

4 In *The Tuning of the World* I rashly quoted John's 'In the beginning was the Word' as if an acoustical vibration had been intended. The present essay is an attempt to locate the antecedents for this idea, which by John's time was more likely accepted as a mute manifestation of divine reason.

5 'Egyptian Myths,' p.5.

The Memphite Ptah is now regarded as the progenitor of the creator-god Atum.

Thus it happened that the heart and tongue gained control over [every] (other) member of the body, by teaching that he [Ptah] is in every body and in every mouth of all gods, all men, [all] cattle, all creeping things, and (everything) that lives ...[6]

The divine act of speaking, which in the Memphite myth is the original creative force, is passed on to all the created creatures, who in their turn are rendered creative.

It is this which causes every completed (concept) to come forth, and it is the tongue which announces what the heart thinks.[7]

In another Egyptian creation myth (from the Bremner-Rhind Papyrus) the creative power of the mouth is emphatically linked with sexual potency.

The All-Lord said, after he had come into being: I am he who came into being as Khepri. When I had come into being, being (itself) came into being, and all beings came into being after I came into being. Many were the beings which came forth from my mouth ...

I planned in my own heart, and there came into being a multitude of forms of beings, the forms of children and the forms of their children. I was the one who copulated with my fist, I masturbated with my hand. Then I spewed with my own mouth: I spat out what was Shu, and I sputtered out what was Tefnut. It was my father Nun who brought them up, and my Eye followed after them since the ages when they were distant from me.[8]

Again the eye follows the voice as the instrument by which the creative act is assessed.

The idea that God's voice created the universe is widespread, and there are numerous echoes of it in other sources. In the Leiden Papyrus we read:

6 Ibid.
7 Ibid.
8 Ibid., p.6

And God laughed seven times: Cha Cha Cha Cha Cha Cha Cha, and as God laughed there arose seven gods.[9]

The similarity between the seven energetic laughs and the seven creative days of Genesis should not go unnoticed. In certain Kabalistic doctrines the whole of creation consists of a gigantic process of divine inhalation and exhalation, a notion that was later picked up by the theosophist H.P. Blavatsky when she wrote: 'The appearance and disappearance of the Universe are pictured as an outbreathing and an inbreathing of the "Great Breath" which is eternal ... When the "Great Breath" is projected, it ... breathes out a thought, as it were, which becomes the Kosmos.'[10]

In the *Pymander* of Hermes Trismegistos, Pymander, 'the mind of the great Lord,' is first perceived as Darkness. Then this Darkness becomes agitated and begins to roar like a fire. Finally 'from out of the Light a holy Word (Logos) came.'[11] Hippolytus (A.D. 170-235), a controversial theologian and champion of the Logos Doctrine during the early days of the Roman Church, reinforces the notion that the uttering of the Divine Word meant physical creation when he wrote: 'But the voice and the name [are] sun and moon.'[12]

Parallels to these themes from the Middle East are found in cultures in other parts of the world. In the Hopi creation myth:

Palongawhoya, travelling throughout the earth, sounded out his call as he was bidden. All the vibrating centers along the earth's axis from pole to pole resounded to his call: the whole earth trembled: the universe quivered in tone. Thus, he made the whole world an instrument of sound, and sound an instrument of carrying messages, resounding praise to the creator of all.

The ancient Mayan creation myth tells how everything began from 'immobility and silence.'

There was nothing brought together, nothing which could make a noise, nor anything which might move, or tremble, or could make noise in the sky.

---

9 *Abraxas*, A. Dietrich, p.17, Pap. J 395.
10 H.P. Blavatsky, *The Secret Doctrine* (Los Angeles, 1974), p. 43.
11 Quoted from Hans Jonas, *The Gnostic Religion* (Boston, 1958), pp. 148-49.
12 *Elenchos*, VI, 13.

Then came the word. Tepeu and Gucumatz came together in the darkness, in the night, and Tepeu and Gucumatz talked together. They talked then, discussing and deliberating; they agreed, they united their words and their thoughts ... Then they planned creation ... Thus they spoke. Let there be light, let there be dawn in the sky and on the earth! There shall be neither glory nor grandeur in our creation and formation until the human being is made, man is formed. So they spoke.

Then the earth was created by them. So it was, in truth, that they created the earth. Earth! they said, and instantly it was made.[13]

The idea that creation proceeded from dialogue rather than monologue is an interesting recognition of the fact that for sound to emerge, two things are necessary: an active and a receptive element. The Maori cosmology also initiates from darkness and silence when Io, the life-force speaks

That He might cease remaining inactive:
'Darkness, become a light-possessing darkness.'
And at once light appeared.
(He) then repeated those self-same words in this manner, –
That he might cease remaining inactive;
'Light, become a darkness-possessing light.'
And again an intense darkness supervened.[14]

The retention of darkness in the Maori myth signifies the continued dependence on instinct even though the cognitive processes have begun to function. Darkness, of course, does not belong to the visible world at all but to the world of listening. The alternation of the two states then indicates that both the instinctive ear and the analytical eye will each serve their purpose, though in the end the world of light will dominate.

Then a third time He spake saying:
'Let there be one darkness above,

13 *Popol Vuh: The Sacred Book of the Ancient Quiché Maya*, trans. D.
    Goetz and S.G. Morley (Norman, Okla.,1950), pp.81-83.
14 'A Maori cosmology,' trans. Hare Hongi, *The Journal of the Polynesian
    Society*, vol. xvi, no.63 (Wellington, Sept. 1907), p.114.

Let there be one darkness below (alternate).
Let there be a darkness unto Tupua,
Let there be a darkness unto Tawhito.
It is darkness overcome and dispelled.
Let there be one light above,
Let there be one light below (alternate).
Let there be a light unto Tupua,
Let there be a light unto Tawhito;
A dominion of light,
A bright light.'
And now a great light prevailed.
(Io) then looked to the waters which compassed him about,
and spake a fourth time, saying:
'Ye waters of Tai-kama, be ye separate.'

To divide the waters is to conquer them, to replace chaos ('darkness, with water everywhere') with the navigable sea and river. To perceive water in separate bodies one is not in water but above it. Water is deprived of its audile-tactile state and will henceforth be visualized from the bridge of the ship and on the navigator's map. The development of consciousness is often illustrated as a movement from the depths of water to dry land. The following text is from the Brahman creation myth as recorded in the *Satapatha-Brahmana*.

Verily, in the beginning this (universe) was water, nothing but a sea of water. The waters desired, 'How can we be reproduced?' They toiled and performed fervid devotions (or, they toiled and became heated). When they were heated, a golden egg was produced. The year, indeed, was not then in existence; this golden egg floated about for as long as the space of a year.[15]

After a year Prajapati emerged from the egg. At the end of another year 'he tried to speak. He said: "*bhuh!*" this (word) became this earth; – "*bhuvah*"; this became this air; – "*svah*"; this became yonder sky.'

We do not know what creation sounded like. It doesn't matter. The voice is its metaphor. It is easier to recognize the formative

---

15 *The Sacred Books of the East*, ed. R. Max Müller (Oxford, 1879 etc.), vol. XLIV, p.12.

power of an incantation in a strange language (*'bhuh!'*) than in one
we understand and can rationalize ('And God said':) but the intention is the same. In all cases creation arises out of the recital of magic
words, uttered with instinctive authority. It may be rough, this
voice-sound, it may be unpredictable and it may be meaningless, for
it is only later given meaning as the thing it produces assumes
definition and can be apprehended by the other senses. The magic
power of such speaking has never been lost; it is present in the recit-
als of so-called primitive people; it is present in ritual incantations
in all religions; it is present in the performances of contemporary
sound poets. The meaning of the magic words is often unknown or
has been forgotten. They are acoustic ejaculations and in them lies
the origin of both language and music. The words of Io, says the
Maori narrator, *'the same words'* are chanted 'in the ritual for
implanting a child in a barren womb.' The invocation of a magic
word is a holy act, however or whenever it occurs. In the
Khândogya-Upanishad we are given directions for reproducing the
sacred word.

1 / Let a man meditate on the syllable Om, called the udgîtha; for the udgîtha
   (a portion of the Sâma-veda) is sung, beginning with Om.
2 / The full account, however, of Om is this: – The essence of all beings is the
   earth, the essence of the earth is water, the essence of water the plants, the
   essence of plants man, the essence of man speech, the essence of speech
   the Rig-veda, the essence of the Rig-veda the Sâma-veda, the essence of the
   Sâma-veda the udgîtha (which is Om).
3 / That udgîtha (Om) is the best of all essences, the highest, deserving the
   highest place, the eighth.
4 / What then is the *Rik*? What is the Sâman? What is the udgîtha? This is the
   question.
5 / The *Rik* indeed is speech. Sâman is breath, the udgîtha is the syllable Om.
   Now speech and breath, or *Rik* and Sâman, form one couple.
6 / And that couple is joined together in the syllable Om. When two people
   come together, they fulfill each other's desire.
7 / Thus he who knowing this, meditates on the syllable (Om), the udgîtha,
   becomes indeed a fulfiller of desires.
8 / That syllable is a syllable of permission, for whenever we permit
   anything, we say Om, yes. Now permission is gratification. He who
   knowing this meditates on the syllable (Om), the udgîtha,

becomes indeed a gratifier of desires.

9 / By that syllable does the threefold knowledge (the sacrifice, more particularly the Soma-sacrifice, as founded on the three Vedas) proceed. When the Adhvaryu priest gives an order, he says Om. When the Hotri priest recites, he says Om. When the Udgâtri priest sings, he says Om, – all for the glory of the syllable. The threefold knowledge (the sacrifice) proceeds by the greatness of that syllable (the vital breath) and by its essence (the oblations).

10 / Now therefore it would seem to follow, that both he who knows this (the true meaning of the syllable Om), and he who does not, perform the same sacrifice. But this is not so, for knowledge and ignorance are different. The sacrifice which a man performs with knowledge, faith, and the Upanishad is more powerful. This is the full account of the syllable Om.[16]

The *Khândogya-Upanishad* is strictly speaking not a cosmogonic myth. Rather it is an attempt to compress the whole of creation into a single comprehensible phenomenon, the sacred sound of the udgîtha Om. The work belongs to the Sâma-veda, and as such it has contributed strongly to the orthodox philosophy of India, the Vedanta. The section quoted is intended to be recited on the occasion of a marriage and is intended as a fertility prayer.

'Let a man meditate on the syllable Om.' It may seem difficult to draw immediate meaning from this statement; but such a meditation, which is to consist of a repetition of the syllable, was intended to draw the thoughts away from all the peripherals of the world and to focus them on the essential issue of existence. The Om, which originally seems to have meant 'yes,' may be conceived as 'the symbol of all speech and life.'[17] In the eighth Khanda the discussion of Om concludes with the question of the origin of the world.

> Then Silaka Sâlâvatya said to Kaikitâyana Dâlbhya:
> 'Let me ask you.'
> 'Ask,' he replied.
> 'What is the origin of the Sâman?' 'Tone (svara),' he replied.

16 *Sacred Books*, vol. I, pp.1-3.
17 Max Müller, in his introduction, ibid., p. xxv.

'What is the origin of tone?' 'Breath,' he replied.
'What is the origin of breath?' 'Food,' he replied.
'What is the origin of food?' 'Water,' he replied.
'What is the origin of water?' 'That world (heaven),' he replied.[18]

Throughout the *Khândogya-Upanishad* we have been made aware that meditation on Om can function as a direct avenue of approach to the gods.

When the sun rises it sings as Udgâtri for the sake of all creation ... This (the breath in the mouth) and that (the Sun) are the same. This is hot and that is hot. This they call svara (sound) and that they call pratyâsvara (reflected sound). Therefore let a man meditate on the udgîtha Om as this and that (as breath and the sun).[19]

The sun pictured here is hardly the sun which in other myths symbolizes the light of knowledge. It is the hot sun, more like the fire images to be introduced in a moment. The purpose of repeating Om is to assist the mind in retracting interest in the phenomenal world, to help it reach a state where the distinctions of consciousness are blurred and ultimately cancelled, a state in which hyperconscious unity is achieved.

Thus we have encountered sound at two important junctures: firstly at the point where the distinctions of consciousness are about to emerge, and secondly at the point where they are about to be erased.[20] The territory that lies beyond these points is the same: it is the unknowable, which Jung and others called the unconscious. The main difference between consciousness and lack of it is between differentiation and non-differentiation. Consciousness knows distinctions, and if evolution means anything, we like to think that these grow ever more subtle; but the unconscious, like its two perfect metaphors, darkness and water, cannot be broken into parts. Sound provides by its rhythm and timing a means of moving from one state to

18 Ibid., p.16.
19 Ibid., p.7.
20 In a sense this is paralleled in our daily experience of waking up and going to sleep where sound also functions on the threshold both in advance of and in conclusion to other sensorial activity.

another, from consciousness to preconsciousness, with the long unified tone drawing us back and the abrupt burst of sound drawing us forward. In a sense sound seems to belong to neither state but hovers on the verge of each. This condition is beautifully dramatized in the Manichean creation myth. Like many other religions, Manicheism recognizes the distinctions of consciousness by a dramatic cosmic dualism between spirit and matter, good and evil, light and darkness. According to Mani's own description, when Primal Man was captured by the Power of Evil, God created The Living Spirit and sent him to the frontier of the region of Darkness. There he made a piercing cry, which found an echo in the ardent response of Primal Man. The call and response became two divine hypostases or persons. The Living Spirit made his way to the region of Darkness and held out his hand to Primal Man, lifting him up again to the region of Light. Thus Primal Man became a model of man's abasement and his salvation, that is, of fractured unity and its restoration. The cry and response dramatically signal the threshold between the two states.

Monotheistic religions differ from polytheistic in their conception of an invisible God. It has been argued that their endurance has been strengthened by this means; what cannot be seen cannot be overturned or subverted. But preserving faith in an invisible God has never been easy, as the trials of Moses with the people of Israel clearly demonstrate. The only way it can be done is to retain God as a vivid acoustic presence. God, whose voice has been withdrawn from creation after the development of consciousness, continues to speak to man via what might be colloquially dubbed as a divine telephone. Usually God calls man in sleep, i.e., when his resistance to pressures from the unconscious is at its lowest. It was in this manner that he conversed with Abraham and Jacob: 'In the dream the angel of God called me: "Jacob!" And I answered: I am here' (Genesis 31:11).

Since Freud we have learned to respect the dream as providing valuable information from the unconscious; or rather we have learned again to respect it for this, since in ancient times the dream was accorded deep significance, and still is among some societies. It was the empiricists who trivialized the dream by regarding the reception of messages from beyond consciousness as illogical and therefore insignificant. Freud and his followers gave the dream back its dignity. Nevertheless there is one startling fact in the dream

interpretations of Freud and his school: they are always interpretations of visual contents. Does the predominantly visual bias of modern life make the dreams of contemporary human beings predominantly visual, or is it only that they have been analysed predominantly in this way? My suspicion is that our dreams are a good deal
more aural than we realize but that because aural experiences are not
susceptible to analysis they are 'translated' into visual terms in the
retelling. I am sure we have all had dreams in which aural experiences figure importantly; the problem is to describe them precisely
enough for interpretation. Aural symbolism is also a poorly developed subject compared to visual symbolism, as it has been developed
by art historians and anthropologists.

The other day I was talking to a young woman about this essay
and she volunteered a recent dream experience that was exclusively
aural in character. She was attempting to repair a rift in her family by
joining tones together; each member of her family was a tone (she
emphatically denied that they were present visually in her dream at
all) and she was attempting to unite the tones in order to achieve harmony. It is difficult to know what Freud or Jung would have made of
such a dream. To begin with they would have to have had a better
knowledge of music than either of them seemed to possess.[21] Psy-
choanalysis is precisely what it claims to be, and as analytical
research it is best, and possibly only, able to function so long as the
material it deals with is visual in nature.

21 Jung's interpretations of the dreams of Miss Miller (see his *Symbols of
Transformation*, volume 5 of the Collected Works) is a good case in point.
Many of Miss Miller's dreams were of acoustic character, and included a
Hymn of Creation that quite remarkably parallels the myths we have
been studying.

> When the Eternal first made Sound
> A myriad ears sprang out to hear,
> And throughout all the Universe
> There rolled an echo deep and clear:
> 'All glory to the God of Sound!'

Jung does not seem to be able to come to terms with this dream in a
satisfactory manner, and when in a later dream Miss Miller reports a
'confusion of sounds, somewhat resembling, "wa-ma, wa-ma,"' Jung's
conjecture is that 'it might, in the context as a whole, be considered a

The vast majority of the 'big' dreams in the Bible are acoustic in nature; rarely do they describe scenes or appearances. Of course the culture of the Bible was aural [22] so we might expect the dreamer to be aurally receptive also; but there is another reason for the aural dream taking precedence over the visual. The heightened sensitivity of the dream state provides the best means for reaching back into the unconscious to receive the renewing and miraculous vitality of Ursound – the creative voice of the Maker. The biblical dream is a soundscape filled with voices – beseeching voices, counselling voices, angry voices.

In his compelling book *The Origin of Consciousness in the Breakdown of the Bicameral Mind* (Boston, 1977) Julian Jaynes argues that before the evolution of consciousness God (or the gods) had direct acoustic presence in the minds of humans as a voice or voices that the hearer blindly obeyed, while with the development of consciousness the voices ceased. The voices originated in the right hemisphere of the brain, opposite Wernicke's area that generates normal speech, and were transmitted by means of the anterior commissure to the left or dominant hemisphere where they were interpreted as divine messages. This state Jaynes calls the bicameral mind. When it atro-

---

slight distortion of the well-known cry "Ma-ma,"' which he uses as a rather arbitrary preface to two lengthy chapters on the mother complex. Such a theme may indeed have been important in Miss Miller's fantasies, and Jung would have been best able to know if it was. What I am saying is that other themes may also have been present which the psychoanalyst was unable to handle.

22 An aural culture is one in which *most* of the important information is received by the ears. This is hard for a visual culture such as ours to comprehend. Even in reading the ancient documents we are constantly being misled by translators substituting visual for aural metaphors and figures of speech. A good example of the type of distortion I am referring to is the following passage (Jeremiah 19:8) which the King James Bible gives with accurate acoustic resonance: 'And I will make this city desolate, and an hissing; every one that passeth thereby shall be astonished and hiss because of all the plagues thereof.' The New English Bible renders this passage inaccurately as a visual image: 'I will make this city a scene of horror and contempt, so that every passer-by will be horror-struck and jeer in contempt at the sight of its wounds.'

phied, the commanding and protecting voices ceased, and man was forced to develop consciousness to protect himself from emergency situations. Jaynes gives numerous examples from historical sources (largely Middle Eastern) in support of the thesis, which is deservedly being taken seriously. Certainly it is supported by the evidence of the Bible, where we discover that while God and Adam converse frequently and openly in the Garden of Eden, after the Fall (consciousness!) it is more often in dreams (or daydreams) that God speaks to man. The God of these dreams is without form. 'You cannot see my face,' he tells Moses, 'for man cannot see me and live' (Exodus 33:20).[23] The formula 'God said to Moses,' which is repeated throughout Exodus and recurs in Leviticus, is a telephone voice; it cannot be seen and it describes no scene. But during this period, that is about 1300 B.C., an interesting transition occurs in the divine voice.

... peals of thunder on the mountain and lightning flashes ... and a loud trumpet blast, and inside the camp all the people trembled ... and the whole mountain shook violently. Louder and louder grew the sound of the trumpet. Moses spoke, and God answered him with peals of thunder ...
(Exodus 19:16ff).

In this passage it will be noticed that while the voice of God is audible to all, it is comprehensible only to Moses. Interpretation of the divine messages is impossible without the assistance of the prophet.

'Speak to us yourself,' they said to Moses, 'and we will listen; but do not let God speak to us, or we shall die' (Exodus 20:19).

This is a pattern with parallels in all prophetic literature: it is present in Zoroastrianism, Mohammedanism (including Sufism), and Manicheism as well as in Judaism and later Christianity. In Zoroastrianism the high priest is called Srosh, which means the

23 The earlier statement (Exodus 33:11) in which it is said 'Yahweh would speak to Moses face to face as a man speaks to God' is assumed to be a later interpolation. In any case it is an isolated instance which is contradicted in all other accounts of Moses' meetings with God.

'genius of hearing'; it is he who hears the divine words and passes them on to the followers. The Manichean community was divided into an 'elect,' who were the priests, and the 'hearers' to whom they explained the dogma. Listening is also an important experience in Sufism. Sāma is the Sufi word for listening. But as the poet Saadi says:

> I will not say, my brothers, what *sāma* is,
> Before I know who the listener is.

The faculty of clairaudience (if I can stretch this term and apply it to the hearing of divine voices) was then something that was drifting away from the majority of men and rested with only a few prophetic spirits during the time Jaynes has identified as the dawn of consciousness, and which he places as late as three thousand years ago. Simultaneously with this withdrawal of divine sound we detect a transformation of the sound-image from that associated with wind and water to that of fire. God first calls to Moses from the burning bush. 'Come no nearer,' God warns. 'At this Moses covered his face, afraid to look at God' (Exodus 3:5-6). There is a great deal of tension here, more than in previous encounters with God. Although fear could have been aroused equally by the water-voice (the Hebrews were profoundly afraid of water), from this point on the fire-voice occurs more frequently than any other in the Bible.

There went up fire out of his nostrils and fire out of his mouth (II Samuel 22:9).

The voice of the Lord scattereth flames of fire (Psalm 29:7).

The name of the Lord cometh from afar, burning in his anger ... his lips are full of indignation and his tongue is a devouring fire (Isaiah 30:27).

Is not my word like as a fire? (Jeremiah 23:29).

The fire voice is passed to the Apostles, occasioning their glossolalia:

And there appeared unto them cloven tongues like as of fire, and it sat upon each of them. And they were all filled with the Holy Ghost, and began to speak with other tongues, as the Spirit gave them utterance (Acts 2:3-4).

The association of mouth, fire and speech is also strong in collo-
quial languages. A person may be 'fired up' or 'inflamed' over something and may make a 'fiery' speech about it. In the Bible, fire is
repeatedly modified by the words 'devouring' or 'consuming,'
reminding us again of the mouth. But the fire-symbol is always one
of extreme panic. More immediate than water, it is best suited to
urgent communication. Since all the voice metaphors for God are
man-made, it is worth pondering the reason for the transition from
the water-voice to the fire-voice, which I think is not adequately
explained by the argument that the Hebrews were not a maritime
people. If it was merely a question of environment the wind could
have survived as a suitable desert voice. Could it be that the more
urgent image was required in a final desperate attempt to summon
up a deity whose voice was receding from man?

In time the voice lifted entirely, leaving a silent god and a weak-
ened religion. For centuries man attempted to reestablish the dialogue by vigorous singing and bell-ringing, but if God answered at all
it was in the silence of the conscience rather than in vivid external
displays. Nevertheless, everything in Christian dogma encourages
the human being to keep ears open in hope that the divine voice may
be heard again. Hearing is the primary action of worship. Eyes are
closed in prayer, which is performed aloud. The priest reads the
words of God and the choir chants them. The sanctus bell speaks for
the presence of the Holy Spirit while the thundering organ remi-
nisces over the earth-shattering theophany on Mount Sinai.

All this would be ridiculous except for one thing: the memory of
Ursound. Somehow we retain a faint acoustic memory trace of God's
ordering and creating presence, even though we cannot grasp it completely. The elements are there – wind, water, fire, thunder, music
and the voice – but that is all we know.

It is enough. For both God and sound are unknowable. If God can
never be weighed or measured or verified in any way, the same may
be said for sound. A visual God is localized in space, seen from an
angle. But an acoustic God is everywhere. This is why the original
metaphors have been so perfectly chosen. Water – in a waterscape
everything is in motion; hearing and touch are the dominant sensations, and vision is practically useless. Wind – God is an invisible
breath-spirit; the wind is heard but has never been seen. In Sumerian,
'lil' means wind and breath, as does 'ruah' in Hebrew and 'pneuma'

in Greek. Darkness – in darkness nothing is localized, nothing has precise value, causing the listener to lean out limitlessly in all directions. Darkness belongs exclusively to the ear. Light is the symbol of knowledge and order, which is why solar deities dominate after the evolution of consciousness; but darkness, like wind, water and fire, is the 'unstable and pregnant reality' from which creation emerges.

Sound is the first force. To make sound is to participate in the original unconscious urge to shape with the voice. The fastest method of getting action is still by speech. This making is instinctive and immediate. Often it is unpredictable. Always it precedes vision. When vision enters it has already ended, as our survey of cosmogonic myths has made clear.

The acoustic God shapes; the visual God analyses. The visual experience is always focused and reflective, which makes it verifiable in ways that sound is not. We fear we have lost this divine force. Desperately we twist everything, hoping that by fixing life for inspection it will return. But the moving force persists elusively. To find it we must return to the waters of instinct and the unshatterable unity of the unconscious, letting the long waves of Ursound sweep us beneath the surface, where, listening blindly to our ancestors and the wild creatures, we will feel it surge within us again, in our speaking and in our music.

2 ACOUSTIC SPACE

As far as I know, the first scholars to use the term 'acoustic space' were Marshall McLuhan and Edmund Carpenter in their magazine *Explorations*, which appeared between 1953 and 1959. There, McLuhan wrote:

Until writing was invented, we lived in acoustic space, where the Eskimo now lives: boundless, directionless, horizonless, the dark of the mind, the world of emotion, primordial intuition, terror. Speech is a social chart of this dark bog.

Speech structures the abyss of mental and acoustic space, shrouding the voice; it is a cosmic, invisible architecture of the human dark. Speak that I may see you.

Writing turned the spotlight on the high, dim Sierras of speech; writing was the visualization of acoustic space. It lit up the dark.[1]

This statement permeates all McLuhan's writings from *The Gutenberg Galaxy* onwards. For McLuhan, the electric world was aural; it moved us back into the acoustic space of preliterate culture. Carpenter developed the theme in *Eskimo Realities*, where 'auditory space' is employed as an interchangeable term:

Auditory space has no favoured focus. It's a sphere without fixed boundaries, space made by the thing itself, not space containing the thing. It is not pictorial space, boxed-in, but dynamic, always in flux, creating its own dimensions moment by moment. It has no fixed boundaries; it is indifferent to background. The eye focuses, pinpoints, abstracts, locating each object in

---

1 Marshall McLuhan and Edmund Carpenter, eds., *Explorations in Communication* (Boston, 1960), p. 207.

physical space, against a background; the ear, however, favours sound from any direction ... I know of no example of an Eskimo describing space primarily in visual terms.[2]

Despite McLuhan and Carpenter's infatuation with the concept, acoustic space did not attract critical attention until the World Soundscape Project was established at Simon Fraser University in 1970. The project's intention was to study all aspects of the changing soundscape to determine how these changes might affect people's thinking and social activities. The project's ultimate aim was to create a new art and science of soundscape design complementary to those in other disciplines dealing with aspects of the visual environment.[3]

Anyone who has tried to hone a new concept for delivery to the public knows how essential it is to find the right tag words to describe it.[4] 'Acoustic space' is too awkward a term to have conferred fame on its inventor. Perhaps one reason is its hybridity,

2 Edmund Carpenter, *Eskimo Realities* (New York, 1973), pp. 35-37.

3 Publications of the World Soundscape Project include R. Murray Schafer, *The Tuning of the World* (New York, 1977); R. Murray Schafer, ed., *The Vancouver Soundscape* (Vancouver, 1978; book and two cassettes); R. Murray Schafer, ed., *Five Village Soundscapes* (Vancouver, 1977; book and five cassettes); R. Murray Schafer, ed., *European Sound Diary* (Vancouver, 1977); Barry Truax, ed., *Handbook for Acoustic Ecology* (Vancouver, 1978). See also, *Sound Heritage*, vol. III, no. 4 (Victoria, 1974), which is devoted to a discussion of the World Soundscape Project; *The Unesco Courier*, November 1976, which is given over to soundscape articles; and Keiko Torigoe, 'A Study of the World Soundscape Project' (Master's thesis, York University, Toronto, 1982).

4 Translation of the word 'soundscape' is a good case in point. The French translation, *le paysage sonore*, has caused little difficulty and is now widely employed. The Poles translated it as *sonosphere* and understood at once what it meant. But when the word was rendered into German originally as *Schwallwelt*, it had little impact. *Klanglandschaft* has also been employed, and when *The Tuning of the World* was translated, soundscape was rendered as *Lautsphäre*. None of these terms seems acceptable to the German mind and as a result there is little interest in the subject in the German-speaking countries.

marking it as transitional, caught between two cultures. The fixity
of the noun 'space' needs something more than the application of
such a restless and vaguely understood modifier as 'acoustic' to suggest the transition from visual into aural culture as McLuhan perceived it. Nor is it easy to subject aural culture to the same system-
atic analysis that has characterized visual thinking. The world of
sound is primarily one of sensation rather than reflection. It is a
world of activities rather than artifacts, and whenever one writes
about sound or tries to graph it, one departs from its essential reality,
often in absurd ways. I recall once attending a conference of acoustical engineers where for several days I saw slides and heard papers on
various aspects of aircraft noise without ever once hearing the sonic
boom that was the object of the conference. This lack of contact is
characteristic of much of the research on sound still, and one aim of
this essay is to show the extent to which considerations with space,
the static element in the title of this essay, have affected the active
element, sound.

When one first tries to conceptualize acoustic space, the geometrical figure that most easily comes to mind is the sphere, as Carpenter evoked it above. One would then argue that a sound propagated
with equal intensity in all directions simultaneously would more or
less fill a volume of this description, weakening towards the perime-
ter until it disappeared altogether at a point that might be called the
acoustic horizon. It is clear at once how many spatial metaphors we
must use to fulfill this notion. In every sense it is a hypothetical
model. In reality, what happens is that sound, being more mysterious than scientists would like to believe, inhabits space rather errati-
cally and enigmatically. First of all, most sounds are not sent travelling omnidirectionally but unidirectionally, the spill away from the
projected direction being more accidental than intentional. Then,
since there is normally less concern with the transmission of sounds
in solids than with their transmission through air, the model should
be corrected to be something more like the hemisphere above ground
level. Experience shows that this hemisphere is distorted in numerous ways as a result of refraction, diffraction, drift and other environmental conditions. Obstructions such as buildings, mountains and
trees cause reverberations, echoes and 'shadows.' In fact, the profile
of any sound under consideration will be quite unique, and a knowledge of the laws of acoustics is probably less effective in explaining

its behaviour than in confounding it. Finally, and most importantly, the sphere described is assumed to be filled by *one sound only*. That is to say, a sound-sphere filled is a dominated space.

The sphere concept may have originated in religion. It is in religions, particularly those stressing a harmonious universe ruled by a benevolent deity, that the circle and the sphere were venerated above all figures. This is evident in Boethius' *Harmony of the Spheres*, in Dante's circles of paradise, and in the mandalas that serve as visual *yantras* in numerous Eastern religions. I will not dwell on this symbolism which, as Jung explained, seems to suggest completion, unity or perfection. The sounding devices used in religious ceremonies such as the Keisu or Keeyzee of Japan and Burma, the temple gongs of India and Tibet, and the church bell of the Western world all retain something of the circle in their physical forms, and by extension their sound may seem to evoke a similar shape.[5]

This circling is quite literally true of the church bell, which defines the parish by its acoustic profile. The advantage of the bell over visual signs such as clockfaces and towers is that it is not restricted by geographical hindrances and can announce itself during both day and darkness. In one of the studies of the Soundscape Project, it was determined that a village church bell in Sweden could be heard across a diameter of fifteen kilometers and there can be little doubt that in past times, given a much quieter ambient environment in the countryside, this kind of outreach was general throughout Christendom.[6] In the late Middle Ages, the intersecting and circumjacent arcs of parish bells quite literally gripped the entire community by the ears, so that when Martin Luther wrote that every European was born into Christendom, he was merely endorsing a circumstance that was in his time unavoidable. Those who could hear the bells were in the parish; those who could not were in the wilderness.

The same thing happened in Islam, which centered on the minaret, from which the voice of the muezzin, often blind, could be heard

---

5 Proust wrote of the sound of the bell as 'oval.' A few years ago, when I had a group of students draw spontaneously to sounds played on tape, the bell was one of the sounds evoking the greatest circularity. The other sound was that of the air conditioner. See R. Murray Schafer, *The Music of the Environment* (Vienna, 1973), p. 21.

6 See *European Sound Diary*, p. 16.

giving the call to prayer. To increase the sounding area, or to maintain it against increasing disturbance, Islam eventually adopted the
loudspeaker, which can be seen throughout the Middle East today,
hanging incongruously from mosaic-studded towers, booming out
over perpetual traffic jams. Like Islam, Christianity was a militant
religion, and as it grew in strength, its bells became larger and more
dominating (the largest of those in Salzburg Cathedral weighs 14,000
kilograms), responding to its imperialistic aspirations for social
power. There can be no doubt that bells were the loudest sounds to
be heard in European and North American cities until the factory
whistles of the Industrial Revolution rose to challenge them. Then a
new profile was incised over the community, ringing the workers'
cottages with a grimier sound.

Returning to Carpenter's definition of acoustic space as 'a sphere
without fixed boundaries, space made by the thing itself, not space
containing the thing,' one notes that the acoustic space here (which
may or may not resemble a sphere) does have fixed boundaries and
does indeed contain something. It contains a proprietor who maintains authority by insistent high-profile sound. That space could be
controlled by sound and enlarged by increasing the intensity of the
sound seems to be an exclusively Western notion, for I can think of
almost no examples of it in other cultures or in antiquity. Lest it be
objected that Buddhist temple bells produce a similar effect, I might
point out that the Buddhist bell is struck by a muted wooden log
rather than a metal clapper, which deepens the sound, perhaps giving
the effect of 'coming from a well,' which is how Sei Shonagon
describes it in *The Pillow Book*.[7] This muting is also evident in language. In Sinhalese, for example, the Buddhist bell is called
gahatáwa while the sharper Christian bell is called *sínāwa*.

It is true that in practically all cultures, religious exercises tend to
be soundful, and in many they are the noisiest exhibitions the society experiences. Whatever the means – sacred bones, rattles, bells or
voices – it is almost as if man is trying to catch the ear of God, to
make God listen. But it is the two most proselytistic religions,
Christianity and Islam, that have shown the greatest desire to
increase the sound output of their acoustic signals, enforcing the
idea that there is no private space in God's world. This point intro-

7 Sei Shonagon, *The Pillow Book*, trans. Ivan Morris (New York, 1967).

Christianity is a militant religion, and throughout history the foundries have been kept busy converting cannons into bells and back again. Source: *The Wood Engravings of Winslow Homer*, New York, 1969.

duces a notion I call the Sacred Noise, which is special in that, unlike other noises that may be subject to prosecution, its proprietor is licensed to make *the loudest noise without censure.*[8] The Sacred Noise originated at a time when the profane world was quiet and the religious world was noisy. In Christian communities, bell ringing was augmented inside the church with voices raised in song, often accompanied by instruments (the organ being the loudest machine produced anywhere prior to the Industrial Revolution). Both inside and out, the church produced the highest sound levels the citizenry experienced short of warfare. Yet no one ever laid a charge against a church for disturbing the peace.

With the outbreak of the Industrial Revolution, the Sacred Noise passed into the hands of new custodians. Then it was the turn of factory owners to establish their social authority by deafening society. It is only after the diminution of its power as a social force that the Sacred Noise becomes an ordinary noise and subject to criticism like any other. Today, the church is weak; therefore, it is possible to criticize church bells, and many communities throughout Europe and North America have recently enacted anti-noise legislation to restrict bell ringing. Similarly, as industrialists come under fire, aural hygienists march into the factories, though the deleterious effects of boilermaker's disease were known from the outbreak of the Industrial Revolution. Today's pluralistic society has thrown up numerous recent contenders for the Sacred Noise, among them the aviation industry, the pop music industry and the police. Here, at least, are three nuclei of social power, all of whom are permitted to celebrate their uncensored presence with deafening weaponry.

Another contender is the community radio station, not perhaps in terms of intensity but rather because of its hectoring insistence to be present at all times and in all places. Since not only the frequency but also the wattage and transmission direction of a radio station is established by regulation, one can witness in charts prepared by broadcasting authorities the most recent model of the unification of a community by sound.[9] One tends to think of radio as an international medium reaching out to gather information from around the

8 See *The Tuning of the World,* pp. 51-52, 76, 114-15, 179, 183.
9 For the sound profile of Vancouver radio stations, see *The Vancouver Soundscape,* p. 40.

world. Of course, this is exactly the potential that it has, but in practice it is scarcely realized. Most of the time radio acts as a magnet with the commercials and announcements drawing listeners from the periphery of the community to the core.

The territorial conquest of space by sound is the expression of visual rather than aural thinking. Sound is then used to demarcate property like a fence or a wall. It stems from the bounded shape of visual perception. For the eye, most objects are bounded, either on the outside like a chair or a tree, or on the inside, like a room or a tunnel. Not only does the notion of bounded shape give us our physical sciences (which are concerned with weights and measures), but it also contributes to the establishment of private property and by extension to the private diary and the private bank account. Once the bounding line becomes a strong perceptual distinction, the whole world begins to take on the appearance of a succession of spaces waiting to be filled with subjects or shattered by vectors. Obviously, this pattern works best where the subject can be fenced off physically (like the king's hunting grounds) or mentally (like university departments). Where it cannot be divided into visual components, sound is driven to assist in demarcation, which is why the parish can be regarded as a steeple plus bells, or a factory as a slum and a whistle.

The only place where sound can be naturally bounded is the interior space, in the cave, which was extended by deliberate design to the crypt, the vault, the temple and the cathedral. The magical sensation of unbroken, sound-filled space is only possible after man moves indoors and begins deliberately to shape his buildings to achieve that sensation. Then, resonant frequencies are used as natural amplifiers to strengthen fundamental tones, and highly reflective materials are sought to extend reverberation time, giving sound a numinosity and amplification quite unlike anything possible *en plein air*. Spoken rhetoric seeks the long vowel, giving rise, for example, to Gregorian chant. In the uniform and continuous spaces of the reverberant hall or stone church, everyone falls into line as performer or listener. One sounding event is made to follow another in resonant sequence and without interruption. All contradictory sounds can finally be pushed out the door into obscurity. When Giedion says, 'this is what one breathes in medieval chambers, quietude and contemplation,' he neglects the astounding resonance of the thriftily-furnished cloister or stateroom, totally unobtainable in the cluttered and cushioned modern interior; and how the echo of these ancient chambers fortified the voice while reading aloud, singing or issuing orders.[10] What Giedion overlooked, McLuhan overheard and sensed how 'a medieval space was furnished when empty, because of its acoustical properties.'[11] Medieval spaces were conceived as oratories. Even the placement of statuary within them was determined in such a way that if the statues could speak, they would be heard to advantage. The diminishment of rhetoric in the modern world may be partly attributed to excessive upholstery which mitigates against the pleasures of eloquent speech, as well as the joy of singing. When architectural historians begin to realize that most ancient buildings were constructed not so much to enclose space as to enshrine sound, a new era in the subject will open out. This pattern is true of Byzantine and Islamic architecture as well as European.

Nourished indoors, the notion of unbroken sound-filled space was later returned to the outdoor soundscape, first in the church bell, later in the factory whistle, then in the radio station, each in turn stencilling its commands on the outside world from a swivel-moored internal power centre.

If indoor space waits silently to be filled with its destined and uncontradicted sound events, outdoor space is a plenum that can never be emptied or stilled. In nature, something is always sounding. Moreover, the rhythms and counterpoints of these soundings interact in dialogue; they never monologue. Who will have the next speech? The frogs may begin, the swallows arrive, geese may fly over, distant dogs may bark at the moon or at wolves. This is the soundscape of my farm, where the orchestration changes every season and every hour. All I can do is listen and try to read the patterns, which is exactly what outdoor people have done for centuries. The influence of sounds on the agrarian calendar has been recorded as far back as Hesiod.

What is true of people living outdoors today was even more true in the primitive societies of the past. In totemic society, the sounds of nature acquired an enlarged meaning as the voices of good and evil spirits whose continued interaction plotted the course of the world.

10 S. Giedion, *Mechanization Takes Command* (New York, 1970), p. 302.
11 Personal communication, December 16, 1974.

All nature resounded with these spirits and everything in nature had its real or implied voice, put there for some purpose by the totemic gods. In fact, the voice of each object was its ultimate indestructible force. Just as the soul of a man was often reckoned as his voice, which escaped him at death in the form of a death rattle, so the sounds of natural objects came and departed mysteriously from the soundscape. But when they were silent, they were still reckoned to be present. They were merely listening to the sounds of other spirits in order to learn their secrets.

'Terror is the normal state of any oral society, for in it everything affects everything all the time.'[12] Like an animal, with ears bristling, man found himself in a world of strange and sudden voices. Spirits inhabited the wind or the cries of birds and insects. Even stones could talk.[13] Which were his friends? Which were his enemies? And how could he exorcise those which possess evil power over him? He listened and he imitated. By the homeopathic reasoning that anyone who can imitate the specific sound of an object is in possession of the magic energy with which that object is charged, primitive man cultivated his vocalizing and his music to influence nature for his own benefit. Marius Schneider writes:

By sound-imitation, the magician can therefore make himself master of the energies of growth, of purification or of music without himself being plant, water, or melody. His art consists first of all in localizing the object in sound and then in coordinating himself with it by trying to hit the right note, that is, the note peculiar to the object concerned.[14]

Much has been written about how the dancer, donning the mask, becomes the thing he represents, taking on its spirit or allowing it to possess him. This fact is equally true for possession by sound, and in an aural society probably even more so. Today, this possession survives faintly in the onomatopoeia of our speech, but more strongly in our creation of music, which is the ultimate transcendence of

12 Marshall McLuhan, *The Gutenberg Galaxy* (Toronto, 1962), p. 32.

13 For examples of talking spirits in nature see, among other sources: Ella Elizabeth Clark, *Indian Legends of Canada* (Toronto, 1960).

14 Marius Schneider, 'Primitive Music,' *The Oxford History of Music* (London, 1957), p.44.

space by sound. For music, freeing itself from objects entirely, moves us quite beyond ourselves and the ordinary, Euclidean geometry of streets and highrises, walls and maps. It is the last kind of sound we really listen to, the last we have allowed to possess us, though most of it today is coalescent with uniformity and imperialism. The heavy amplification of rock music has more in common with the noise profiles of heavy technology in sustaining the grip of Western impe-rialism than it does with the subtle musical diversions practised by aural cultures. The ethnomusicologist could provide many useful examples to support that distinction. Steven Feld, for instance, tells how Kaluli tribesmen, imitating birds, quite deliberately refrain from synchronizing their drumming because birds never sing in uni-son.[15] The *aperçu* that the sound world possesses a million unsyn-chronized centres is illustrative of the consciousness I am trying to describe.

Aside from the area inhabited at the moment, spatial apprehen-sion by non-literate peoples everywhere is vague, for everything over the hill or beyond the forest is hidden. Here, sound becomes light, making the hidden visible. The cataract down the river is heard by the canoeist before it is seen, as the Leatherstocking novels of James Fenimore Cooper repeatedly demonstrate. The horn is the only straight line in the forest. News of the distant world is received by a messenger, who often announces his approach by means of special sounds, for instance the horns of the old postal coaches or the bells worn by the runners of Kublai Khan.[16] In the countryside any inva-sion by a stranger is tracked by barking dogs. So it was in the days of the *Kalevala* and still remains today.

> Still the castle-dog was barking,
> And the yard-dog still was barking,
> And the furious whelp was baying,
> And the island watch-dog howling,
> Sitting by the furthest cornfield,
> And his tail was briskly wagging.

15 Personal communication. For an amplification of this subject, see: Steven Feld, *Sound and Sentiment: Birds Weeping, Poetics and Song in Kaluli Expression* (Philadelphia, 1982).
16 Marco Polo, *Travels* (Atlanta, Ga., 1948), p. 154.

Then again said Pohja's Master,
'Not for nought the dog is barking,
Never has be barked for nothing,
Never growls he at the fir-trees.'
So he went to reconnoitre ... [17]

Where geography was impassable or extra speed was required,
messages were sent over long distances in code. One thinks of the
talking drums of Africa or the trumpet communications between
armies. When Roland put his Olifant to his lips, 'thirty great leagues
the sound went echoing.'[18] Swiss alphornists still converse across
miles of silent valleys. In the Middle East it was the great copper
drums, sounded by the *chaouches*. Bells tell the shepherd and herdsman the location and condition of their sheep and cattle, and silent
caravans signal their advance by the same means.

Out of the black darkness is heard the distant boom of a heavy bell.
Mournfully, and with perfect regularity of iteration, it sounds, gradually
swelling nearer and louder, and perhaps mingling with the tones of smaller
bells, signalling the rearguard of the same caravan. The big bell is the insignia
and alarum of the leading camel alone. But nearer and louder as the sound
becomes, not another sound, and not a visible object appears to accompany it.
Suddenly, and without the slightest warning, there looms out of the darkness,
like the apparition of a phantom ship, the form of the captain of the caravan.
His spongy tread sounds softly on the smooth sand, and like a great string of
linked ghouls, the silent procession stalks by and is swallowed up in the
night.[19]

The Aborigines of Australia practised the art of listening to the
ground to pick up the arrival of invaders, just as we used to listen to
the rails to learn if a train was coming. An Indian hunter tells how he
tracks a moose:

17 *Kalevala*, Runo xviii, lines 525-35, trans. W.F. Kirby (London, 1907),
   p. 206.
18 That would be about ninety miles! *The Song of Roland*, trans. Dorothy L.
   Sayers (Harmondsworth, Middlesex, 1971), p. 119.
19 Lord Curzon, *Persia and the Persian Question* (London, 1892), vol.1,
   p.275.

He is out of sight, but I put my ear to a tree in the forest, and that brings me
the sound, and I hear when the moose makes his next leap and I follow ... I
follow always, listening now and with my ear against a tree.[20]

Today we have forgotten how to listen to the earth, but it was
once widely practised. On June 17, 1776, a slave heard the Battle of
Bunker Hill at a distance of 129 miles by putting his ear to the
ground.[21] The aural man learns that the world beyond his vision is
crisscrossed with information tracks. Where I live, for instance, a
hunter on the runway can tell by tracing the bark of his dog whether
he is in pursuit of a deer or a rabbit; the deer runs in a straight line
and the rabbit in a circle.

In aural cultures, the right position for settlement is often
influenced by whether warning signals can be properly heard. When
the Indians of Canada were numerous and threatening, the fields laid
out by the first white settlers along the St. Lawrence were narrow,
with habitations at one end. Families could shout warnings across
to one another and congregate to defend themselves. We may com-
pare this pattern to the larger and squarer fields of Upper Canada and
the North American West, surveyed after the Indians had become
peaceable. A book on Charlemagne tells how the ninth-century
Huns constructed their habitations in rings so that news could be
voiced quickly from farm to farm, with the distance between the
rings being determined by the outreach of a warning trumpet.[22] And
from Marco Polo, one learns that in the city of Kin-sai, great wooden
drums on mounds of earth were beaten by guards and watchmen to
telegraph emergencies.[23]

20 'Hunting the Moose' (told by Big Thunder) in Natalie Curtis, *The Indians'*
   Book (New York, 1987), p.11.
21 Recorded in C.C. Bombaugh, *Oddities and Curiosities* (New York, 1961),
   p.280. The same source records that guns fired in Stockholm in 1685 to
   announce a death in the royal family were heard 180 miles away, and that
   the cannonade of a battle between the English and the Dutch in 1672 was
   heard in Shrewsbury and Wales, a distance of about 200 miles from the
   scene of the action.
22 Notker the Stammerer, *Life of Charlemagne*, trans. Lewis Thorpe
   (Harmondsworth, Middlesex, 1969), p.136.
23 Marco Polo, *Travels*, p.232.

I have given these numerous examples to show how space enters the consciousness of aural society. Here, sound may transpierce space, animate space, evoke space or transcend space but never to the exclusion of contradictory transients. Defining space *by* sound is very different from dominating space *with* sound. When sound articulates and denotes space (as it does for the blind person, or as it does at night, or as it did and does for any group of people in a forest or jungle) the perceptual emphasis is subtly shifted into the aural modality, so that we discover we are discussing something that might better be called 'spatial acoustics' – as if distant sounds, close sounds, sounds up and sounds down were merely a few of the demonstratives that could be used to describe how the sound world imparts its many meanings to us.

When the forests of eastern North America were dense – and they are in places still dense enough to sense the accuracy of what I am about to say – anyone living in them relied essentially on the ear and the nose for information beyond the six-foot range their eyes would carry them. The ear remained continually alert, just as one observes it today among animals. To survive in such a world, people have to learn to respect silence, or at least have to know how to participate in the pattern of give and take, sounding when it is safe or unsafe and listening between times to know when to do so.

In aural societies many professions depend on acute listening. A mechanic knows the sound of a smooth-running engine just as a baker knows when the bread is baked by its hollow tap. Watermelons and coconuts are also tapped to determine ripeness. In India, a row of pots is checked by running a stick across them; and a wagoner used to check for split spokes in the same manner. European glassmakers still check the resonance of crystal by tapping it; and I have been told of a Scottish stonemason who could tell if there was a fissure in a stone by moving his watch over the far surface and listening to the ticking.

'Speak that I may see you,' said blind Isaac to Jacob. But the unblind Eskimo says the same today.[24] And I have been shown by the natives of northern Argentina how they sing to the mountains 'to bring them to life.' It is in sounds that the world becomes palpable and complete. Without them the earth is barren and its objects

24 Carpenter, *Eskimo Realities*, p.33.

remain 'hidden'. Then the post horn or the train whistle is the sound that comes from far away (that is to say, it carries the symbolism of distance and travel wherever or whenever it is heard), just as the storyteller's voice is the sound that comes from long ago. And the lover's voice kisses the air near one, and the child's laughter echoes into the future. Extension and duration acquire an immediacy that visual experience can neither emulate nor even suggest.

Seeing and sounding are different. Seeing is analytical and reflective. Sounding is active and generative. God spoke first, and saw that it was good second. Among creators, sounding always precedes seeing, just as among the created, hearing precedes vision. It was that way with the first creatures on earth and still is with each newborn baby. For a projected publication (which never materialized), I once asked McLuhan to write an article on acoustic space. The manuscript I received was 'Changing Concepts of Space in an Electronic Age,' where acoustic space was characterized as 'a simultaneous field of relations ... its centre is everywhere and its horizon nowhere.' In a letter he embellished this point, which is synonymous with the earlier cultures I have detailed, and which may be a fair comment on the culture we are today retrieving:

We are living in an acoustic age for the first time in centuries, and by that I mean that the electric environment is simultaneous. Hearing is structured by the experience of picking up information from all directions at once. For this reason, even the telegraph gave to news the simultaneous character which created the 'mosaic' press of disconnected events under a single dateline. At this moment, the entire planet exists in that form of instant but discontinuous co-presence of everything.[25]

At the outset, I called acoustic space a transitional term, touching on two cultures, but in a sense unnatural to each. In the one, everything sounds and has its sound presence, but like a spirit, incorporeal, without precise extension or shape. In the other, this resonating life is beaten down, first in the inner spaces of the church, the concert hall and the factory; then, by extension, through the external soundscape. In the past, it was the parish; today it is broadcasting that conquers space with sound. The first form will be more difficult

25 Personal communication, December 16, 1974.

for indoor man to comprehend, as he hides today behind glass windows listening to the radio and peering out at the silent cacophony of the streets. Glass shattered the human sensorium. It divided the visually perceived world from its aural, tactile and olfactory accompaniments. Or rather, it substituted new accompaniments to the accentuated habit of looking. Until this situation is corrected, all thinking about the phenomenal world will remain speculative in the literal sense of the word.

THREE DOCUMENTARY STUDIES

How can we study the soundscapes that existed before the invention of tape recorders and measuring instruments? In *The Tuning of the World* I spoke of the value of earwitness descriptions by individuals who listened carefully to the environments in which they lived. While such descriptions may lack technical accuracy, they make up for it by giving us personal opinions and reflections on the sounds described – and that is something microphones never do. The following three vignettes of widely varying soundscapes by a painter and two authors are examples of the kind of research I was advocating. They exemplify very different types of soundscapes, as the titles suggest.

THE DIALECTICAL SOUNDSCAPE

There is no sound in the split second in which pictorial images live. But sound can be implied by movement, and the greater the variety and energy of movement, the more resonant the pictorial surface becomes. Among the painters of the Renaissance, one whose canvasses vibrate not only with sounds but often also with smells and tastes (food is frequently in evidence) is Pieter Brueghel; and thus it is that where all other documents fail, we are able to sense something of the acoustic life of sixteenth-century Flemish towns and countryside by making inventories of the sound events suggested by his paintings.

In *The Battle Between Carnival and Lent* (1559) we are presented with the soundscape transformation that occurred at Shrovetide (the three days prior to Ash Wednesday). Two processions are confronting one another, the one consisting of Carnival's boisterous followers, costumed and playing homemade instruments, and the other a Lenten procession of children, nuns, priests and beggars which, while more austere, is by no means silent.

Source: Kunsthistorisches Museum, Vienna. Used by permission.

Two symbolic buildings frame the painting: the Blue Ship Tavern on the left and the church on the right. Other houses make up the background. The houses are of no great height; the streets are wide and the large town square is unpaved, all of which suggests a dry rather than a resonant setting, suitable therefore for the great variety of conflicting events with which the town is populated. All buildings appear to be made of brick and wood except for the church, which is of stone. The sounds of the square seem to have pierced the secular buildings drawing spectators (auditors) to the open windows. None of the interior spaces of these buildings achieves any identity. The case of the church is different. The doors are open and the interior darkness suggests a powerful resonance that seems to be flowing out of the edifice, clinging to the black gowns of the departing penitents.

The square contains well over one hundred people of all ages, some happy, some miserable and some silent. Those whose mouths are open widest are the beggars and cripples, and the painting contains quite a number of them. Strangely there are few animals present. I count only two: a pig behind the well in the centre and a bird in a cage hanging on the outside of the house at the top left of the painting (cirlced on page 51). There are no dogs, no cats, no flying birds. This is emphatically a human soundscape.

The Spirit of Carnival is mounted on a wine barrel, which is on skids, pushed by his followers. He has his foot in a pot, attached to a string, so that he may be kicking it against the barrel. His followers, who are dressed in bizarre costumes, are making a racket on an assortment of instruments. We can distinguish a woman with a friction drum, a man knocking two (tin?) cups together, a woman scraping a knife across a grate, a lute player with a metal pot on his head, and a masked figure with what appears to be a hand clapper. Two other characters, the dwarf in front and the woman behind, have respectively a spoon and a pan mounted in their headgear, which could be noisemakers.

The Spirit of Lent is a lean old hag on a wagon dragged along by a priest and a woman. (This is one of two wooden-wheeled wagons in the picture.) Note that Lent is wearing wooden clogs. Behind her, several children are carrying what appear to be wooden clackers or wood blocks. We remember that during Lent no church bells are rung, their sound being replaced by wooden ratchets. No bells are in evidence in the painting nor are there any metal noisemakers in the Lenten procession. I spoke of the resonance that the nuns seem to be carrying out of the church, but of course this is an illusion; the nuns are not singing. The only real sound associated with the church are the prayers of several kneeling figures who have taken their positions under arches in order that their petitions might receive favourable amplification.

There are two pieces of street theatre in progress. Before the Blue Ship Tavern a group is performing a skit that has been identified as *De vuile Bruid* (The Dirty Bride). In this group we notice a man with a mock guitar consisting of a coal shovel and a knife.

Outside the house in the top left corner another group of players is performing the mascarade of *Ourson and Valentin*, watched from within the house by a group of spectators.

Several groups of children are at play. In the upper right a group are playing with tops. There are seven tops in the picture and four are in motion. While all are activated by strings, there are three distinct shapes providing (we assume) at least three distinct tonalities when spun.

To the left, a group of older children is playing a game of pot-throwing. One clay pot lies shattered on the ground and another seems on its way down.

Behind this group another is skipping in a circle. Probably a rhythmic song accompanies their dance.

There are other groups of citizens in the picture, one of the most conspicuous being the group of cripples with their wooden crutches (and open mouths) in the centre of the square. The precise sounds of other activities remain uncertain except for those of the musicians. A bagpipe player is seen (upper centre), and in the extreme centre background a man plays a transverse flute accompanied by a drummer, though this is nearly imperceptible.

The entire picture is alive with sounds, and each of the leading players has his or her own identifying noisemaker. Yet, though there is conflict, there is no disorder. No one is protesting the noise, and no single sound is dominating or is likely to dominate the scene. It is a scene with as many acoustic centres as there are activities. Nothing is hi-fi here. Every sound is heard in the presence of others. The essential vitality is in the dialectic of the sounds, and the excitement and satisfaction for the listener is in overhearing as much as hearing.

There are quiet zones in the picture. All four corners are quiet; but so is the centre where a figure dressed as a fool is seen leading off a couple (whose backs are toward us). The light tones of the ground about this trio make them the focal point of the painting; the most frenzied activities are deflected from a mute centre, further evidence that although we are witnessing a busy soundscape the painter is not implying a noisy one.

Yet there is, so to speak, a fundamental tonality to this soundscape, and aside from human vocal activity it is one character-ized by its dominant material: wood. Our inventory has revealed wooden tops, wooden wheels and skids, wooden barrels, wooden doors and windows, a wooden ladder, wooden crutches, wooden tables and chairs, wooden clappers, wooden buckets and even a fire of wood. Every soundscape is characterized by its predominant materials, but a real appreciation of that statement would have to await the comparison of Brueghel's painting with another document that is materially quite different.

THE CLOSED
SOUNDSCAPE

In Book VI of the 'Cosette' section of *Les Misérables*, Victor Hugo gives us a good description of what we might call a closed soundscape, one turning in on itself and admitting no extraneous distractions, like a musical composition. The scene is the commun-ity of Bernardines of the Obedience of Martin Verga, a strict order of nuns, sheltered behind eighteen-foot walls at No. 62 Petite Rue Picpus in the centre of Paris. The date is 1815. I have drawn a picture of the enclosure (p.54) from Hugo's extensive description. The story of how Jean Valjean and Cosette come to live at the convent need not detain us.

Hugo dramatizes the impenetrability of the place by telling us that without knowledge of the password, no entry beyond the porter's gate was permitted. After repeating the password one was allowed to ascend a narrow stairway to a little room. At one side was a grating and a tape attached to a bell.

If you pulled this tape, a bell tinkled and a voice was heard, very near you, which startled you: 'Who is there?' asked the voice.

It was a woman's voice, a gentle voice, so gentle it was mournful.

Here again there was a magic word which you must know. If you did not know it, the voice was heard no more, and the wall again became silent as if the wild obscurity of the sepulchre had been on the other side.

Assuming you did know the magic word and were allowed to enter, you would discover a complex of buildings around a central garden, each with its own characteristic sounds.

At one corner was the old convent chapel where the nuns observed the seven canonical hours of the Church, beginning with matins, held daily from 1:00 to 3:00 a.m. The nuns chanted the offices in a 'pure, plain chant, and always in a loud voice for the whole duration of the office ... For the office of the dead they take so low a pitch that it is difficult for female voices to reach it. The effect is thrilling and tragical.' Occasionally there were public services in the chapel. When this happened the nuns were hidden behind a seven-foot curtain. 'When the nuns were attending offices in which their rules commanded silence the public was advised of their presence only by the sound of the rising and falling stall seats.'

The Bernardines of Martin Verga observed the rule of silence every Friday. 'This rule of silence had the effect that, in the whole convent, speech was withdrawn from human creatures and given to inanimate objects. Sometimes it was the church-bell that spoke, sometimes the gardener's.' The gardener's bell was tied about his knee and sounded everywhere he went as a warning to the nuns of his presence.

The Little Convent, also situated in a corner of the grounds, was inhabited by elderly nuns of various orders whose convents had been destroyed during the Revolution. Hugo calls them a 'motley' community compared to the Bernardines, who inhabited the cells of the Old Convent along the opposite wall of the complex, and whose lives were regulated by strict formalities.

They live in open cells. When they meet one another, one says: 'Praise and adoration to the most holy sacrament of the altar.' The other responds: 'Forever.' The same ceremony when one knocks at another's door. Hardly is the door touched when a gentle voice is heard from the other side, hastily

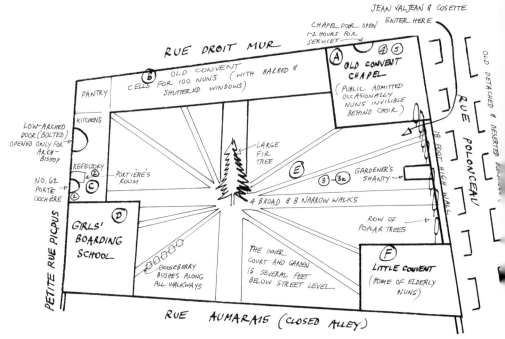

JEAN VALJEAN & COSETTE

CHAPEL DOOR OPEN   ENTER HERE
1–2 HOURS FOR
SERVICES

RUE DROIT MUR

PANTRY

OLD CONVENT CELLS FOR 100 NUNS (WITH BARRED & SHUTTERED WINDOWS)

Ⓐ OLD CONVENT CHAPEL
(PUBLIC ADMITTED OCCASIONALLY NUNS INVISIBLE BEHIND CHOIR)

KITCHENS

LOW-ARCHED DOOR (BOLTED) OPENED ONLY FOR ARCH-BISHOP

REFECTORY

NO. 62 PORTE COCHÈRE

PORTIÈRE'S ROOM

LARGE FIR TREE

4 BROAD & 8 NARROW WALKS

Ⓔ

GARDENER'S SHANTY

18 FOOT HIGH WALL

RUE POLONCEAU

OLD DETACHED & DESERTED BUILDINGS

GIRLS' BOARDING SCHOOL

PETITE RUE PICPUS

GOOSEBERRY BUSHES ALONG ALL WALKWAYS

THE INNER COURT AND GARDEN IS SEVERAL FEET BELOW STREET LEVEL

ROW OF POPLAR TREES

Ⓕ LITTLE CONVENT
(HOME OF ELDERLY NUNS)

RUE AUMARAIS (CLOSED ALLEY)

Diagram of The Bernardine Convent at 62 Petite Rue Picpus, Paris, around 1815, according to Victor Hugo's description in Book vi 'Cosette' of *Les Misérables*.

saying: 'Forever!' Like all rituals, this becomes mechanical from habit, and one sometimes says 'forever' before the other has had time to say, what is indeed rather lengthy, 'Praise and adoration to the most holy sacrament of the altar!'

The same phrase is repeated by the entire community after the three bells signalling each hour of the day.

Of quite a different character is the girls' boarding school in the other corner of the complex. During recess they were allowed into the garden.

After the chants, the bell-ringing, the knells and the offices, all at once this hum of little girls burst forth sweeter than the hum of bees. The hive of joy opened and each one brought her honey. They played, they called to one another, they formed groups, they ran; pretty little white teeth chattered in the corners; veils from a distance watched over the laughter, shadows spying the sunshine; but what matter! They sparkled and they laughed. These four dismal walls had their moment of bewilderment.

The timetable of the Bernardine community was punctuated with absolute regularity by a galaxy of bells. Let us make an inventory of them (see the numbers on the map).

1 / The door bell at the *porte cochère*, already mentioned.
2 / The Portress's 'very sonorous' summons bell, 'a kind of acoustic telegraph' by which individuals could be called to the locutory. 'Each person and each thing had its special ring. The prioress had one and one; the sub-prioress, one and two. Six-five announced the recitation, so that the pupils never said going to recitation, but going to six-five. Four-four was Mme de Genlis's signal. It was heard very often ... Nineteen strokes announced a great event. It was the opening of the *close door*, a fearful iron plate bristling with bolts which turned upon its hinges only before the archbishop.'
3 / The gardener's knee bell. 'It resembled the dimly heard tinkling of cow-bells in the pastures at night ... the sound of the bell followed every movement of the man. When the man approached, the sound approached; when he moved away the sound moved away: if he made some sudden motion a trill accompanied the motion; when he stopped, the noise ceased.' After Jean Valjean is taken on as an assistant gardener, 'two little bells were heard tinkling in the corner of the garden ... Immense event!'
4 / The chapel bell. 'At each hour of the day three supplementary strokes sound from the bell of the convent church. At this signal prioress, mothers, professed nuns, sister servants, novices, postulants, all break off from what they are saying, doing or thinking and say at once, if it is five o'clock, for example: "At five o'clock, and at all times, praise and adoration to the most holy sacrament of the altar!" If it is eight o'clock: "At eight o'clock and at all times," etc., and so on, according to whatever hour it may be.'
5 / A death in the convent is announced by a special bell. 'A single stroke of a bell was heard. "The nun is dead," said he. "There is the knell." And he motioned to Jean Valjean to listen. The bell sounded a second time ... The bell will strike every minute for twenty-four hours until the body goes out of the church.'

6/ There were other bells: one to tell the porter to summon the physician, another when the physician departed, and still another, 'a complicated ringing ... for the mothers. They always hold a chapter when anybody dies.'

The predominant sounding material of the convent of the Obedience of Martin Verga was bronze. It clanged day and night throughout the year except at Lent, when, as in Brueghel's time, it would have been replaced by the sounding of wooden ratchets with, one may imagine, astonishing effect. Hugo doesn't mention this but we accept the description as far as it goes, for Hugo was a faithful earwitness chronicler, even when his ear appeared to play tricks on him. As proof we pass to the late novel *Ninety-three*, where we find an old man (could be Hugo) standing on a Brittany beach at twilight when his attention is attracted by an unusual sight.

He was looking at the steeple of Cormeray, directly in front of him beyond the plain. Indeed, something extraordinary was taking place in this steeple.

The outline of this steeple was clearly defined; the tower could be seen, surmounted by the spire, and between the tower and the spire, the belfry, square, without screen, and open on all four sides, according to the style of Breton bell towers.

But this belfry appeared alternately open and closed at regular intervals; its lofty window showed all white, then all black; the sky could be seen through, then it was seen no longer; it would be light, then eclipsed, and the opening and shutting followed each other a second apart, with the regularity of a hammer on an anvil.

This steeple in Cormeray was about two leagues away in front of the old man; just about as far to his right on the horizon he saw the steeple of Baguer-Pican; the belfry of this steeple was opening and shutting in the same way as that in Cormeray.

He looked to his left at the steeple of Tanis; the belfry of the tower at Tanis was opening and shutting just the same as that at Baguer-Pican ...

What did it all mean?

It signified that all the bells were ringing.

To appear and disappear in this way they must be pulled furiously.

What was it then? evidently the tocsin.

They were sounding the alarm, sounding it frantically, sounding it everywhere, in all the belfries, in every parish, in every village, and not a sound reached his ears ...

All these bells madly calling from every side, and at the same time, silence; nothing could be more weird.

The old man looked and listened.

He did not hear the tocsin, but he saw it.

The tocsin, alarm bell of the French Revolution, rendered mute by the offshore wind of evening. The tocsin, soon to silence the bells of all churches and monasteries, and return them to the foundries to be smelted into cannons. The tocsin, bizarrely introduced by the writer of genius, as - silence.

THE OPEN SOUNDSCAPE

Anton Chekhov's novella *The Steppe* is a fictionalized account of a journey made by the author as a child across the Ukrainian steppe during a July heat wave. Rich in acoustic detail, both described and implied, it exemplifies a soundscape once familiar to many but now quite exotic for most. The journey, which lasts several days, is built over two recurring keynotes, like the tonic and dominant of a musical composition. The tonic is provided by the sounds of nature and the dominant by the rumbling wagon carrying the travellers.

It rattled and creaked at every movement; the pail, hanging on behind, chimed in gruffly, and from these sounds alone and from the wretched rags of leather hanging loose about its peeling body one could judge of its decrepit age and readiness to drop to pieces.[1] (p.161)

Here is a sound, or to be more precise, a vibration, that will accompany the travellers each day, infecting their speech the way clothes dictate behaviour: comments are choppy, thoughts desultory and observations haphazard. When the wagon stops, the squeaky accompaniment lifts away to a natural soundscape of wide dimen-

---

[1] All quotations are from the Constance Garnett translation of 'The Steppe,' in volume 7 of *The Tales of Chekhov* (New York, 1985).

sions, sometimes arranged by the author in tiers: close, mid-distance and far. For example:

Stillness reigned. There was no sound except the munching and snorting of the horses and the snoring of the sleepers; somewhere far away a lapwing wailed, and from time to time there sounded the shrill cries of the tree snipe who had flown up to see whether their uninvited visitors had gone away; the rivulet babbled, lisping softly, but all these sounds did not break the stillness, did not stir the stagnation, but, on the contrary, lulled all nature to slumber. (p.176)

Like the wagon, the soundscape of the steppe is also loose-jointed; the only synchronized sound is that of a row of mowers, their scythes moving together in unison: 'Vzhee, vzhee.' Dogs bark intermittently, announcing the approach of the strangers in a manner familiar to countryside dwellers the world over. It is a soundscape of near and far, the far becoming nearer and the near receding in a hazy fluctuation as the wagon passes. In any soundscape there will be stationary sounds, moving sounds and sounds moving with the participant, but in Chekhov's account everything seems to be drifting up to the limitless sky. When a woman sings some distance away, the sound source cannot be localized, due to the effect of the heat waves on the stagnant midday air.

Somewhere at a distance a woman was singing; and it was difficult to tell where and in what direction. The song was subdued, dreary and melancholy, like a dirge, and hardly audible, and seemed to come first from the right, then from the left, then from above, and then from underground, as though an unseen spirit were hovering over the steppe and singing. Yegorushka looked about him, and could not make out where the strange song came from. Then as he listened he began to fancy that the grass was singing ... it began to seem as though this dreary, mournful song made the air hotter, more suffocating and more stagnant ... (pp.178-79)

Occasionally small events are magnified at close range, as when the child, Yegorushka (Chekhov), catches a grasshopper and holds it for a long time in cupped hands, 'listening to the creature playing on its instrument.' Crickets, locusts and birds, these are like the woodwind notes in Chekhov's orchestration.

Arctic petrels flew across the road with joyful cries; marmots called to one another in the grass. Somewhere, far away to the left, lapwings uttered their plaintive notes. A covey of partridges, scared by the chaise, fluttered up and with their soft 'trrr!' flew off to the hills. In the grass crickets, locusts and grasshoppers kept up their churring, monotonous music. (p.166)

Other voices in the orchestration: lapwings, rooks, corncrakes, bustards, a hawk. Chekhov displays the countryman's knowledge of birdsong.

Corncrakes and quails do not call in the July nights, the nightingale does not sing in the woodland marsh. (p.210)

The circadian change of night-sounds is dramatic on the steppe.

A gay youthful twitter rises up from it, such as is not heard by day; chirruping, twittering, whistling, scratching, the basses, tenors and sopranos of the steppe all mingle in an incessant, monotonous roar of sound in which it is sweet to brood on memories and sorrows. The monotonous twitter soothes to sleep like a lullaby; you drive and feel you are falling asleep, but suddenly there comes the abrupt agitated cry of a wakeful bird, or a vague sound like a voice crying out in wonder 'A-ah, a-ah!' and slumber closes one's eyelids again. Or you drive by a little creek where there are bushes and hear the bird, called by the steppe dwellers 'the sleeper,' call 'Asleep, asleep, asleep!' while another laughs or breaks into trills of hysterical weeping – that is the owl. (p.210)

Because of the darkness in which all sounds are surprises, those heard at night affect the listener in a much more emotional way than those heard by day.

In the churring of insects … in the flight of the nightbird, in everything you see and hear, triumphant beauty, youth, the fulness of power, and the passionate thirst for life begin to be apparent; the soul responds to the call of her lovely austere fatherland, and longs to fly over the steppes with the nightbird. And in the triumph of beauty, in the exuberance of happiness you are conscious of yearning and grief, as though the steppe knew she was solitary, knew that her wealth and her inspiration were wasted for the world, not glorified in song, not wanted by anyone; and through

the joyful clamour one hears her mournful, hopeless call for singers, singers!
(p.212)

There is always an unfinished quality to Chekhov's descriptions
of nature, prompting early Russian critics to call him an 'impression-
ist.' So it is that water enters the novella unobtrusively, as a hint
only, though eventually it will form the climax of the story. On the
first day out, the travellers pause by a stream. Like any continuous
sound, it seems to retard the passage of time. 'The rivulet gurgled
monotonously, the horses munched, and time dragged on endlessly
...' (p.181) Several days pass before water is encountered again, this
time it is a 'quiet, modest little river,' that resounds with 'snorting
and splashing' as the travellers plunge in for a swim. The third water
event is a violent storm occupying six pages of vivid description in
which sound, for the first time in the novella, becomes violent. The
event is announced by distant thunder:

There was a sound as though someone very far away were walking over an
iron roof, probably barefoot, for the iron gave a hollow rumble. (p.272)

The wind enters and surges to the forefront:

The wind dashed whistling over the steppe, whirled round in disorder and
raised such an uproar from the grass that neither the thunder nor the creaking
of the wheels could be heard. (p.273)

Rain follows, at first as a 'quiet, regular sound' then beginning to
prattle 'like two magpies.' Thunder and lightning follow:

Suddenly, exactly over his head, the sky cracked with a fearful deafening din;
... the sky was not growling and rumbling now, but uttering short crashing
sounds like the crackling of dry wood. 'Trrah! tah! tah! tah!' the thunder rang
out distinctly, rolled over the sky, seemed to stumble, and somewhere by the
foremost waggons or far behind to fall with an abrupt angry 'Trrra! ... Trrah!
tah! tah!' floated over his head, rolled under the waggons and exploded 'Kraa!'
(pp.275-76)

The three water events are widely spaced in the story, but anyone
who has travelled an arid landscape for several days will sense their

importance, not merely as refreshing punctuations of the journey, but as the focal points shaping the entire story.

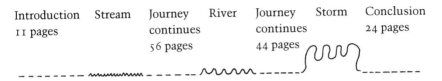

Introduction	Stream	Journey	River	Journey	Storm	Conclusion
11 pages		continues		continues		24 pages
		56 pages		44 pages		

Reaching the final destination, a small city where Yegorushka is to attend school, speaking is normalized, the voices cease shouting and are almost hushed, for the boy has caught cold in the storm and is put to bed. The arrival is a coda; the real climax is the storm. We are reminded that in sparsely-populated environments everywhere the most authoritative voices are those of nature, and humans are reduced to listeners, sifting the information of the elements to determine how it may affect their welfare. They come from near and from far, these voices, but especially from far; and this is how the open soundscape distinguishes itself from the closed soundscape of the urban dweller, where everything is close, dense and at times confusing. Today all sounds must have 'presence' to be heard, and the microphones used in music, broadcasting and telephones intensify this presence. Vision has been transformed in the same way as higher and higher buildings screen off the horizon. We have lost the habit of distant listening and have entered a new era in the history of sensory awareness. About the same time as Chekhov was writing, Sir Richard Burton, surveying the desert near Cairo, spoke of the felicity of 'sounds sweetened by distance.' The poetry of such sounds is what distinguishes *The Steppe* from the sound chronicles of most contemporary urban authors.

4

THREE REFLECTIONS

THE DECEPTIVE SOUNDSCAPE

During one of the less invigorating periods of my life, I spent two years living in a coach house at the back of a property on Warren Road in Toronto, in an area of the city referred to by its inhabitants somewhat wistfully as Lower Forest Hill – though the real mansions of Forest Hill began north of St. Clair Avenue. Nevertheless it was still considered 'a very good address' by people who know Toronto and have a genuine respect for those areas endowed with old money.

It is a neighbourhood of large houses, large gardens and very large and beautiful old maple and chestnut trees. Nearby stands Casa Loma, Toronto's *Neuschwanstein*, built by a Toronto millionaire early in the twentieth century, not, alas, in honour of an artist as mad King Ludwig's palace had been, and with the hope that Wagner might one day come to live in it, no, without such noble intentions. It was built merely to gild the millionaire before the high society of Toronto. He went bankrupt before completing it.

It was in the shadow, as it were, of this manifestation of misguided plutocracy that I found my coach house in the garden of a very nice doctor. Its seclusion attracted me, and I was desperate to find a quiet place to live for as long as I might be forced to endure the city. Here at least, I thought, I could be insulated in a large thick-walled old room in winter, and camouflaged in a corner of the secret garden in summer.

As it turned out, the area is actually much noisier than many other parts of Toronto. The large century-old houses need frequent repairs. Many of them are now passing from their original families to new owners, who wish to make significant changes: sun porches, family rooms, larger windows, landscaping. There are even instances of people buying houses only to flatten them and totally rebuild. This means that the neighbourhood suffers continuous construction noise, which everyone tolerates knowing that their turn will be next. You can hardly complain about a neighbour's backhoe when you are waiting the arrival of your own cement mixer.

The roots of the old trees often get into the city's sewer system, and the branches interfere with the telephone and hydro lines. Frequently whole trees have to be taken out limb by limb in order not to destroy anyone's property, an activity that can keep a chain-saw crew occupied for a week.

These are sounds unexperienced in other areas of the city where the vegetation is less developed or nonexistent. Other sounds are different too: for instance, swimming pools. I used to be able to see four swimming pools from my Lower Forest Hill window. In each case large old trees had been rooted out to make room for them. The rustling of leaves was replaced all summer long by the competing hums of these pools. Added to this was the hefty vibration of countless air conditioners – for everyone had them.

Such sounds would be less pronounced in new suburbs. I used to notice this on visits to my brother's house in Markham. In a new development there is little road or sewer repair work to be done. The owners have not yet grown tired of their homes and have not yet begun to remodel them. There are few swimming pools; they will come after the mortgages are paid off.

Another difference between suburb and city is in the operations of gardening. Both have power lawn mowers, but while everyone in the suburbs cuts his own grass, in Lower Forest Hill no one did. They had Portuguese or Greek gardeners who arrived often at 7:30 a.m. and went from one lawn to the next right up the street finishing at about noon. This timetable contrasts with the suburbs, when lawns are cut after work or on weekends.

I might mention in passing that there is no reason for a society to call itself 'advanced' when it has declined to silence the power lawn mower since its inception in the 1950s. The price of one ticket to a concert or the theatre, added to the cost of a lawn mower, could equip it with a muffler sufficient to reduce its noise emission by twenty decibels.

One instrument professional gardeners possess, which has not yet made its way to the private arsenal, is the leaf blower. Leaf blowers are among the most stupid inventions of modern civilization. It is debatable whether they clear leaves and grass better than a rake; it is certain they are destroying the hearing of the operators. Only a brutish society would allow itself to be awakened each morning to such inorganic noises as these without a murmur of protest. Gone is the careful shaping of vegetation that once marked the gardener's art, as the grass is shaved, flowers are chopped, and anything else lying around is shredded, then the debris is blown about in circles in a vague attempt to make piles of it.

The characteristic sound of raking the autumn leaves has been totally replaced in Lower Forest Hill by this howling. And there is an abundance of leaves from the large old trees to make mighty work for the little men who have been commissioned to get rid of them. I used to notice how they would frequently drive up in their trucks in the late afternoon to step out and blow the leaves off the driveways so that their patrons would have a nice, clean place to park when they came home from the office.

Such operations must, of course, be performed daily from early October until the first snowfall when the snowplows take over. The old autumnal smell of burning leaves, so strong in my memory, has been replaced by the city's trucks with huge nozzles and an incredible scream, circulating through the streets to suck up the leaves and pulp them.

Autumn is also a time for draining the swimming pools. To accomplish this, men used to come around with pumps that roared continuously for three hours. The reverse occurred in May when they cleaned and filled the pools. These two sounds framed the summer in Lower Forest Hill as faithfully as the flocks of migrating Canada geese frame the seasons of the rural soundscape.

In the winter one was a little better protected from the noise, first of all because cold Canadian winters necessitate more insulation in the construction of buildings and also because the weather tends to keep people indoors. I recall Marshall McLuhan's statement that Northerners go home to be with company and go out to be alone, whereas Southerners go home to be alone and go out to celebrate.

Traditionally, the Northern soundscape became quieter in the winter with the hibernation of animals and insects and the migration of
birds. Perhaps this bred the misanthropy we recognize among Northern writers and artists, in the Russians, in the Germans and Scandi-
navians. It is present in Canada too, and is evident in the work of our
painters and poets; but it would no longer be true to say that the winter is quieter unless one's refuge is beyond the playground of drunk
or giddy snowmobilers.

Fortunately there were no snowmobiles on Warren Road, but
there were snowplows. Generally they arrived in the middle of the
night when there were few parked cars to impede their work. Often
they came together with a fleet of trucks lined up, motors on the run,
waiting to carry the snowpiles off to some remote dump on the other
side of town. Once I was treated to an exhibition of 'Metromelt' – for
such was the name proudly stencilled on the bulwarks of this enormous tank of a machine. Its function was to scoop up the snow and
melt it in an enormous roaring oven, then eliminate it in the direction of storm sewers, which smaller plows were attempting to keep
open. But the water promptly froze and turned the roads into rinks. I
never saw Metromelt again, though I imagine my taxes went on paying for it for years.

There were many other characteristic sounds in that part of the
city, variations that distinguished it from other areas. The majority
of dogs seemed to be large, as if they were kept as guard dogs. They
would bark at about 8:00 a.m. when their owners let them out, for
none of them seemed to stay out all night. Since their owners went
off to work by nine and would not consider 'disturbing the neighbourhood' by leaving their dogs to bark all day, they presumably put
them back inside before they left. The other times one heard the
dogs was at about 10:30 p.m. when they were taken out for their evening walks. One rarely heard a dog barking all evening because of the
owner going off to a party – an occurrence common in lower-class or
country environments.

I was also surprised at first not to hear children playing in the
yards or on the street. This was only partly due to the restrained
behaviour of the residents; it was also because most children in this
neighbourhood were programmed to strict timetables, leaving little
time for play. I would see them dropped off by their private-school
buses and immediately driven off again by their mothers to a music

lesson, a dance lesson or the tennis club. Or else they would enter their cavernous houses to work on school assignments or to play with their computers. Sometimes they would come out into their backyards and listen to the radio. But they always kept it at a low volume, usually tuned to middle-of-the-road stations. And only occasionally would a neighbourhood party spill out over the block to keep one awake all night.

Altogether it was a deceptive neighbourhood, quiet and respectful on one level, while on another it was far more ferocious than many other parts of the city. The noises were part of the technological transformation experienced by all older parts of Toronto as decaying properties are upgraded and rotting utilities are renewed.

But Lower Forest Hill is only one of many deceptive soundscapes encountered in modern life. Think, for instance, of how real estate is sold, often from pictures or a quick visit to the property under consideration. No time to sense the rhythms of the place; no time to learn about noisy neighbours or future developments that could totally transform the acoustic environment. Or think of how vacations are advertised: a few flashy pictures of a beach with smiling, sleek-bodied yuppies drinking tequila. It's not until you get there that you experience the twelve-lane expressway on the other side of the hotel or have to contend with the continuous bedlam of the holiday music and partying. We live in a world advertised for the eye. Even the food rarely tastes as good as it looks in the picture.

What amazed me about the inhabitants of Lower Forest Hill was their evident faith that since money procures, among other things, peace and quiet, they had acquired that condition by buying into the best part of town. They thought they had acquired 'royal silence as absolute monarchs dwell in,' and seemed dead scared to admit they were stuck in a sonic slum.

THE GLAZED SOUNDSCAPE

In the Tunisian restaurant in Montreal, the proprietor and his wife share a carafe of wine fitted with a spout from which they pour the

The way in which materials are used provides soundscape character. The sounds of water are different in rural India than in modern urban plumbing. Source: *South Asia*, B.L.C. Heineman, London, 1969.

The plank streets, sidewalks and houses of Vancouver conditioned its soundscape before the city advanced to cement, metal and glass. Source: Vancouver City Archives.

wine directly into their mouths by raising and tipping it, in exactly the way the old wineskin would have worked. The sensation of drinking is entirely different when the liquid is squirted into the mouth rather than sipped out of a glass or sucked through a straw, and so are the accompanying sounds, on this occasion a bright burbling as the air seeks to replace the liquid through the twisted thin spout. Nothing touches the mouth but the liquid. It is probably the purest way to drink, yet it has been replaced by the glass as individual proprietorship has replaced tribal sharing. Slurping liquids through straws from bottles or cans represents an even greater degree of privatization – the hidden elixir. The glass, replacing more tuneful receptacles, is raised and chimed at the beginning of the meal, partly in compensation for mute consumption, an exercise denied its prophylactic successor, the plastic cup. Materials change, sounds change, social customs change.

The soundscape of every society is conditioned by the predominant materials from which it is constructed. Thus we may speak of bamboo, wood, metal, glass, or plastic cultures, meaning that these materials produce a repertoire of sounds of specific resonance when touched by active agents, by humans or wind or water. The containers and conveyances for water could make a nice dossier of keynote sounds for cross-cultural study. In modern times water forms a strong domestic keynote in the presence of taps, toilets and showers; in other cultures the sounds of water are more clearly marked at the village fountain or pump where all washing is done and from which all water is drawn to the household.

Unlike water, stone does not make a sound on its own; rather only when brushed, chipped, scraped or crushed. The various methods in which this happens have characterized cultures in many parts of the world. Before roads began to be macadamized in the nineteenth century, wagon wheels over cobblestones provided one of the clearest keynotes of all stone cultures, often rising to the level of annoyance, so that straw was often spread over the roads near hospitals or around the homes of the sick to mute the sound of the horses' hooves and the grating of the wagon wheels.[1] Europe was a stone cul-

---

1 There are numerous allusions to this European literature, for instance in chapter 19 of Thackeray's *Vanity Fair* where the street is laid knee deep in straw and the knocker of the door is removed when Miss Crawley is ill.

ture and to a large extent still is, particularly in its smaller, less-touched communities. When stones were piled up to build cathedrals, palaces and homes, they affected the reflection of sounds both within and without their surfaces, fortifying spoken rhetoric and amplifying music and military parades. North America was originally a wood culture, passing, like modern Europe, to cement and glass during the twentieth century.

Glass is the most imperceptible soundscape material and therefore needs special treatment. Its history goes back possibly nine thousand years or more,[2] though its prominence is much more recent. About 200 B.C. Roman glassmakers learned how to roll out slabs of glass to make mosaics and also to close small window surfaces, though their semi-opacity admitted only feeble light. The manufacturing of glass was improved by the Venetians after 1300 but it was not until the seventeenth century that the glazing of windows began on a large scale. In 1567 Jean Carré, a merchant from Antwerp, had received a twenty-one-year license from Queen Elizabeth I for making window glass in Britain, but it was Louis Lucas de Nehan's new method of casting in 1688 that for the first time permitted the production of large polished plates of flat glass of relatively uniform thickness from which it was possible to make excellent mirrors and fill large window openings.

For a long time there was a tax on glazed windows. In Britain the occupier of a house with ten windows had to pay an annual tax of 8s.4d. in 1776, rising to £2.16.0 in 1808. The high rate continued until 1825 when the tax was halved and houses with seven or fewer windows were declared exempt. When the excise duties on glass were repealed in 1845 the industry immediately entered a period of rapid growth. A symbol of its triumph was the Crystal Palace of 1851, containing a million square feet of glass.

During the twentieth century the commercial streets of all cities have gradually suffered their romantic stone work to be chipped away to provide larger display windows, while above them tower buildings that have altogether abolished windows, replacing them with skins of glass. From the streets we are given views of interiors

2 According to Sir W.M. Flinders Petrie, glaze was known from 12,000 B.C. in ancient Egypt, though the earliest pure glass dates from 7,000 B.C. See: G.W. Morey, *The Properties of Glass* (New York, 1938), p.12.

The glazed windows of the eighteenth century may actually have increased urban noise by attempting to shut it out. 'The Enraged Musician,' from *The Works of William Hogarth*, vol. 1, London, n.d.

once private and mysterious; from the towers, executives contemplate the skyline and envision distant goals and objectives. None of this is new. We have lived with it for some time. Our concern is with the change of perception brought about by glazing.

The glazed window was an invention of great importance for the soundscape, framing external events in an unnatural phantom-like 'silence.' The diminution of sound transmission, while not immediate and occurring only gradually with the thickening of glazing, not only created the notion of a 'here' and a 'there' or a 'beyond,' but also introduced a fission of the senses. Today one can look at one's environment, while hearing another, with a durable film separating the two. Plate glass shattered the sensorium, replacing it with contradictory visual and aural impressions.

With indoor living, two things developed antonymously: the high art of music, and noise pollution – for the noises were the sounds that were kept outside. After art music had moved indoors, street music became an object of particular scorn. Hogarth's celebrated print *The Enraged Musician* shows the conflict in full view. A professional musician indoors clamps his hands over his ears in agony while outside his workroom a multitude of sonorous activities are in progress: a baby is screaming, a man is sharpening knives on a grindstone, children are playing with ratchets and drums, several hawkers are selling wares assisted by bells and horns, and one shabbily-dressed beggar has targeted the musician's window for an oboe serenade. The developing antagonism between music and the soundscape can be more clearly sensed by comparing Hogarth's print with Brueghel's town square of a century earlier. Hogarth's print contains glass windows. Brueghel's painting does not. Brueghel's people have come to the open windows to listen; Hogarth's musician has come to the window to shut it.

In a study of fairy tales, Marie-Louise von Franz points out that glass 'cuts you off, as far as your animal activity is concerned ... Mentally you are not cut off. You can look at everything through glass practically undisturbed, for you can see as well as though it were not there ... but it cuts off the animal contact ... People very often say, "It feels as if there were a glass wall ... between me and my surroundings." That means: "I see perfectly well what is going on, I can talk to people, but the animal and feeling contact, the warmth contact is cut off by a glass wall ..."'[3] The world of sounds and textures, the palpitating, kinetic world, is zoned out; we still watch it move, but from our (generally seated) position indoors our physical contact with it has ceased. The physical world is 'there'; the world of reflection and speculation is 'here.' Without our participation 'there' tends to become: a) deserted (as around modern apartment houses); or b) squalid (as in dense urban areas); or c) romanticized (as from a resort window).

One could actually argue that noise in the city increases in accordance with the thickness of glazing. The beautiful French windows along the eighteenth- and nineteenth-century avenues of European

3 Marie-Louise von Franz, *Individuation in Fairy Tales* (Boston and London, 1990), p.15.

cities, now frosted over as their prosperous former tenants desert them for quieter residences, document how such windows, sufficient at one time to resist street noise, have long since become inadequate. Those windows were intended to be opened; they did not seal off the environment totally as do the unopenable windows of the modern hotel room.

When the space within is totally insulated it craves reorchestration: this is the era of Muzak and of the radio, a form of interior decoration, designed or absent-mindedly introduced to reenergize the space and render it more sensorally complete. Now the interior and exterior can become totally contradictory. The world seen through the window is like the world of a movie set with the radio as soundtrack. I recall travelling in the dome car of a train passing through the Rocky Mountains with schmaltzy music on the public address system and thinking: this is a travelogue movie about the Rocky Mountains – we are not here at all.

When the division between 'here' and 'there' is complete, the glass wall will become as impenetrable as the stone wall. Even thieves will respect it. Shattered glass is a trauma everyone is anxious to avoid. 'He shall rule them with a rod and shatter them like crockery,' is a potent acoustic image in Revelation (2:27). A keynote of the Middle-Eastern soundscape under normal circumstances, crockery became a violent signal when broken. For us the same is true of glass. And yet one cannot help feeling that the mind-body split of the Western world will only be healed when some of the glass in which we have sheathed our lives is shattered, allowing us again to inhabit a world in which all the senses interact instead of being ranked in opposition.

THE CROWDED SOUNDSCAPE

During those occasional times when I am in a city with nothing to do in the evening I sometimes switch on the hotel television set to watch the news. As I never watch TV at home, I am always struck by the pictures, in particular by the magnitude of crowds that have been in the news so frequently in recent years. At one time a potent crowd could be relatively small; it took only eight thousand shop-keepers and artisans to storm the Bastille and initiate the French Revolution. But to have half a hope of accomplishing its mission today, a crowd seems to require half a million or more aroused citizens. Of course, the world population is growing quickly – it is expected to quadruple between 1950 and 2050, according to UN statistics – and the wide-angle lens of the TV camera gives us a lively spectacle of what is happening. But the grandeur of crowds comes across better in image than in sound. We see them from a helicopter or a rooftop as a seething mass behind the reporter's voice, but we only hear them long enough to convince us that their congregation is really newsworthy and never with the full-frequencied yawp of a true multitude.

This is only partly owing to the limitations of the TV loud-speaker; it is also a matter of attitude, or to be more precise, a matter of fear. Liberal democracies have good reason to be frightened of the mob because liberal democracies function best as an assembly of minorities with varying points of view. The crowd, drawn together for one purpose, has only one voice. That is its threat to democracy, that barbaric bawl, that inflexible demand, that single roaring proclamation.

The crowd question will become increasingly significant in the decades to come. Elias Canetti analyses it in detail in *Crowds and Power*, cataloguing types of crowds and discussing the psychology behind crowd formation and dispersal. I am particularly interested here in the acoustical phenomenon, the very phenomenon we are rarely allowed to sense in the media. At the beginning of his book, Canetti emphasizes the importance of touch in any crowd situation.

It is only in a crowd that man can become free of his fear of being touched. That is the only situation in which the fear changes into its opposite. The crowd he needs is the dense crowd, in which body is pressed to body; a crowd, too, whose physical constitution is also dense, or compact, so that he no longer notices who it is that presses against him.[4]

4 Elias Canetti, *Crowds and Power* (New York, 1981),
   pp. 15-16.

Touch and sound are intimately connected; in the lower frequencies tactility and sounding meet as the pedal tone breaks into a vibrating pulse. This intimacy encourages the densely-packed crowd to invoke sound as its most potent weapon. In every other way it is vulnerable to penetration and disunification by better-armed opponents who seek to neutralize it from outside. It is primarily with its voice that it defends itself and seeks to remain invincible. The crowd roars, the crowd chants, the crowd screams – you don't count the voices; there is only one voice. If it contains within its membership individuals who have not entirely surrendered to its purpose by the encouragement of touching, sound will reinforce the dedication of the wavering.

I think it was in *The Arrow in the Blue* that Arthur Koestler described his final conversion to communism while singing 'The International' in a crowd, after all his self-debating on the subject had produced no firm decision. Similarly, there is a passage in St. Augustine's *Confessions* where the fate of a man who had forsworn gladiatorial shows is sealed after he had reentered the maelstrom of a crowd. 'If only he could have stopped his ears!'[5] cries St. Augustine despairingly.

There are many ways of characterizing a crowd, by its purpose, its credo or its numbers; this is what the explainers, the media men and the politicians, try to do. But vocally the crowd is beyond all understanding. How many nuances are detectable in its bawling? Joy … anger … exasperation … derision … rudimentary emotions, at times chaotic but more often unified rhythmically in the repetition of slogans, for unless the crowd speaks with rhythmic incisiveness it can be fractured, set upon itself internally and be routed.

The principal means of expression is the voice; but there are other mechanisms also. For instance, the Shiite Muslims 'form their right hand into a kind of shell and violently and rhythmically beat themselves with it beneath the left shoulder. A hollow sound ensues, produced by many hands simultaneously, which can be heard at a distance and is very effective.'[6] Military crowds used to beat their swords or spears on their shields in a similar manner or, using their shields as resonators, shouted into them to produce an even greater

---

5 *The Confessions of St. Augustine*, VI.
6 Canetti, *Crowds and Power*, p.176.

din. By this din armies sought to intoxicate themselves with power, and military chronicles contain accounts of battles won by the noise of an army alone.

The military crowds of the twentieth century helped to transform speech into a set of aggressive, throbbing proclamations. Source: Heinz Hohne, *The Order of the Death's Head*, New York, 1969.

In any noisy situation vocal utterances must be clipped and paratactic, like military commands. By the early twentieth century urban noise had increased to a point where it began to affect writers in a similar way, and among the first were the Futurists, led by F.T. Marinetti. 'Through a disjointed, feverish, and posturing language Marinetti was able to capture something of the mood of a human crowd in motion ...' This is István Anhalt commenting on Marinetti's rhetoric in a book in which he shows parallel developments in twentieth-century music. Marinetti's prose is 'the text of a poster, a proclamation, or a series of headlines. It is a throbbing, aggressive, insistent language, brooking no dissent, dismissing the need for reflection, intolerant, and destructive.'[7] In his *Manifesto of Futurism* Marinetti had proclaimed: 'We will sing of great crowds excited by work, by pleasure, and by riot; we will sing of the multicoloured, polyphonic tides of revolution in the modern capitals.'[8]

The influence of these crowd-choirs is conspicuous in much contemporary music, first of all in the bloated orchestras of Berg and Schoenberg, then later in the statistical organization of Xenakis' works, as well as the cluster and aggregate effects of Ligeti and the 'mob' vocal outbursts of Lutoslawski and other members of the Polish school. Crowd power is everywhere present in rock music, which could not exist without it. 'No one goes to a rock concert unless they're stoned or stupid,' a teenager tells me, and yet almost everyone has been there. And the music ricochets from car radios and ghetto blasters through the streets over the back yard fences and dribbles out of the Walkman of the passenger next to you on the bus, where no one speaks, and you realize that music is the glue of the modern multiracial, multilinguistic city, holding it together more effectively than any political or social system, and you allow yourself to hope that it will continue to do so, fearing the consequences if it fails. Without having experienced them, you can believe that there are more violent forms of intolerance than the tyranny of the loudspeaker.

I once met an Italian who was involved in a comparative study of the speech intonations of Mussolini and Hitler: the precise use of anacrusis and downbeat, the suspensions, the timing of exclamation

7 István Anhalt, *Alternative Voices* (Toronto, 1984), p.9.
8 *Marinetti: Selected Writings*, ed. R.W. Flint (London, 1972), p.42.

points and question marks – all the tricks of demagoguery to keep the crowd hypnotized. The microphone adds another dimension to the arousing and stilling of a multitude. The classical politician likes to hear his voice booming through the public square, so that even when he speaks indoors he shouts at the microphone, which is placed some distance from him in order to pick up reverberation as a reinforcing feedback loop. You can still hear such politicians in Eastern Europe or Latin America where their appearances on radio and television are generally prefaced with band music.

The style is also favoured by academics, as I learned during a conference on 'New Dimensions in Communication' held in Buenos Aires in April 1992, during a violent autumn storm. Under a corrugated steel roof against which the rain beat like a thousand Gatling guns, half a dozen professors took turns shouting at a microphone before a crowd of five hundred confused students. When it was my turn to speak I suggested we listen to the storm for a while since nothing else could be heard anyway, but the microphone was too tempting an object to be left unmanned for long, and someone soon resumed shouting at it while a thousand ears leaned forward, desperately trying to distinguish the syllables from the spit.

By contrast the politician in more advanced democracies prefers his voice to be close-miked to still the anxieties of his audience; he tries to get into the same room with you, reassuring you like a long-time family friend. (Often a script is in evidence giving an additional semblance of reasonableness to the scene.) The classic politician needed the crowd and developed skills to manipulate it; the modern politician designs his rhetoric to prevent crowd-formation.

Britain provides an interesting anomaly, for in British Parliament we are allowed to hear the yea- and nay-sayers, often in noisy confrontation. This is because the British Parliament dates back to a time of aural rhetoric rather than scripted speeches, a feature uniting it with Periclean Athens as well as consensus democracies everywhere. Here is Tacitus speaking of the German tribes in the first century A.D.

When the assembled crowd thinks fit, they take their seats fully armed.
Silence is then commanded by the priests, who on such occasions have power to enforce obedience. Then such hearing is given to the king or state-chief as his age, rank, military distinction, or eloquence can secure – more because his

advice carries weight than because he has the power to command. If a proposal displeases them, the people shout their dissent; if they approve, they clash their spears. To express approbation with their weapons is their most complimentary way of showing agreement.[9]

In ancient times assemblies were often held on a rock, the solidity of the meeting place giving firmness to the decisions reached. Everyone was in attendance. To raise one's voice in such assemblies did not necessarily indicate anger, but merely dramatized the magnitude of the issue under discussion – the way we often raise our voice today on an intercontinental telephone call. In those days society was often defined by the outreach of the (unamplified) human voice. We recall that Plato's ideal republic was to consist of five thousand people because a greater number would make it impossible to hear the orator.

'Do you know Vézélay?' General de Gaulle once asked André Malraux. 'How did the knights below hear the voice of St. Bernard, who spoke quite without a microphone?'[10] The date was March 31, 1146, when St. Bernard preached to an estimated one hundred thousand knights and soldiers to launch the Second Crusade from a knoll on the north side of the hill of Vézélay. The knoll is still there, marked by a cross beneath which a large sloping field has been preserved. It is here that the assembly presumably gathered. What is interesting acoustically (and de Gaulle seems to have known it) is that the listeners were below the speaker. Normally one would expect sound waves to rise – the reason amphitheatres are ranked upwards. As I recall, the Pnyx, where the Athenian assembly met, also slopes downward from the speaker's rostrum; but the average number of citizens in attendance has been estimated at not more than two to three thousand. The Areopagus in Athens was also a hill where speeches were given. St. Paul preached there but evidently to a small crowd.[11] His speech is preserved but the text of St. Bernard's is lost. Words diminish in importance as the multitude grows.

Wouldn't the situation have been more like the meetings Gandhi

---

9 Tacitus, *The Agricola and the Germania*, translated by M. Mattingly and revised by S.A. Handford (Harmondsworth, Middlesex, 1970), p.111.

10 André Malraux, *Les chênes qu'on abat ...* (Paris, 1971), p.36.

11 Canetti, *Crowds and Power*, p.42.

The hill at Vézelay, France, where St. Bernard preached the Second Crusade to an assembly of 100,000 knights and soldiers in 1146. Question: How did they hear him? Source: Magazin du Pélerin, Vézélay.

held with audiences of similar magnitude, where the listeners knew the text already and were there to feel the *darshan* or aura of the speaker rather than his precise words?

Writing in the wake of Nazism, Canetti devotes few paragraphs to the silent crowd: the crowd of the candlelight vigil, of the peaceful marches protesting the nuclear arms buildup, the religious crowd 'standing together before God,' or the crowd struck dumb at the scene of a disaster. Perhaps the memory of the holocaust was too immediate for him. But the silent crowd deserves attention, and, in an increasingly crowded world, it may be our only hope before we all succumb to bedlam.

When modern humanity gave up life in the country for life in the city, when it deserted open spaces for the dense packing of the megalopolis, when the alarm clock replaced the sunrise, and factory noise obliterated wind, rain and the birds, when the drowsiness of natural life was surrendered to the mad dash to get ahead, the frictions of increased human contact, the hell of other people, as Sartre put it, replaced the great geo-botanic garden that had been the scene of past existence and the quiet life it promoted. Has it been extinguished from memory or can a new ecological awareness help to recover it? Can exercises in individual and, above all, collective meditation bring back the contemplative life as an antidote to the formation of ever greater and more dissatisfied crowds? Spiritual leaders have been working tirelessly to instill this consciousness, and today there are signs that therapists of all kinds, and even some educators and artists, are beginning to join them.

What we seem to need are rituals of tranquillity in which large assemblies of people could feel the serenity of a shared experience without the desire to proclaim their emotions in destructive or disfiguring action. In this sense we might again study the model of the Western concert audience to determine whether it might have wider or evolving significance. When we think about it, how astonishing is the concert audience, quietly sitting before the music, scarcely breathing, engulfed by the mysterious vibrations in the air about them. I suppose every piece of music longs to be worshipped in silence, but few achieve such a distinction, and some achieve it only by the authority of habit rather than the privilege of beauty. I have often wondered whether the ritual of the concert couldn't be transposed to other environments and transformed into a collective contemplation of a dawn bird chorus, a summer solstice or an Earth Day celebration.

I'll leave it there, with a flitting thought of another silent crowd, that of the billions upon billions of spermatozoa rushing blindly every second towards their goal of sustaining and increasing human life on the planet.

5 THE CANADIAN SOUNDSCAPE

In 1974 or thereabouts I suggested that the Canadian Broadcasting Corporation might consider the call of the loon as a spacer between its programs. I thought the CBC needed space to counteract the impression that all their programs were produced in little donut-shaped rooms by the dwarfs of Niebelheim. Of course, no one paid any attention to the suggestion, and ever since the programs have been connected by electronic twitters engineered by arrangers whose inspirations hover somewhere between their crotch and their armpit.

But if one wanted a natural sound to represent Canada, that of the common loon would be most appropriate, for it makes both its summer and winter home in Canada. Variants familiar to northern listeners are the red-throated loon, the Arctic loon and the yellow-billed loon. The loon is not a U.S. citizen; it does not pass the winter in Florida or Hawaii, nor is it heard in Brazil, Somalia or Korea. The call of the common loon is a truly uncounterfeiting and uncounterfeitable soundmark of Canada. It is recognized by all Canadians who have spent time at cottages or have undertaken canoe trips during summer months and belongs to that select class of natural utterances that once heard will never be forgotten. The call consists of two parts: a slow, haunting yodel and a maniacal laugh that can make a listener's hair stand on end by its suddenness and its resemblance to a woman's voice. I used it as the model for the unaccompanied Princess's aria in *The Princess of the Stars*, where it floats across the lake at the opening and close of the work. *Princess* is probably the most 'Canadian' work I've written, if by Canadian one means something that authentically reflects the habit of living in a place one knows and loves.

All accurate descriptions of sound will be biographical, based on

personal experience. Anything otherwise would be romantic or illu-
sionary. Therefore, all I can do in these pages is to track a few of the
many sounds that have been close to me in the parts of Canada I
have known.

My parents came from the Prairies of Manitoba, and as a child I
used to spend the summer vacations on my grandfather's farm. I
remember the endless squeaking of the windmill and the droning of
the combines as the wheat was harvested. In a cart pulled by a pony, I
used to ride out to the men in the fields, taking them their dinner, for
they worked almost ceaselessly during harvest. Sometimes we
would go horseback riding in the evenings, and although the sound
of horses' hooves was not new to me (bread and milk were still
delivered by horse-drawn wagons in all Canadian cities in those
days), the pounding of unshod hooves on the Prairie turf made the
most vivid impression, probably because it reminded me of cowboy
movies. Years later, when I read Frederick Philip Grove's *Over Prairie Trails*, that sound came back to me, for Grove's book describes
trips he made each week from his home to the school where he was a
teacher, twenty-five miles away, in summer in a horse-drawn buggy
and in winter in a sleigh. Often the trips were made by night or in fog
or during a winter storm. Navigation was then by ear rather than eye.

A rumbling sound made me sit up at last. We were crossing the 'twelve-mile
bridge.' In spite of my dreaming I was keeping my eyes on the look-out for
any sign of a landmark, but this was the only one I had known so far, and it
came through the ear not the eye.
    I had become all ear. Even though my buggy was silent and though the
road was coated with a thin film of soft clay-mud, I could distinctly hear by
the muffled thud of the horses' hoofs on the ground that they were running
over a grade.
    I listened intently for the horses' thump. Yes, there was that muffled hoof-
beat again – I was on the last grade that led to the angling road across the
corner of the marsh ... [1]

Grove lived at Rapid City, a few miles from my grandfather's
farm. The most startling memory I have from my childhood sum-
mers there is the slam of the screen door on the kitchen, a sound I

---

[1] Frederick Philip Grove, *Over Prairie Trails* (Toronto, 1951), p.34.

have heard repeatedly all my life, all across Canada and almost nowhere else. That coil spring must have been sold to three-quarters of the rural households of Canada, becoming the most prevalent domestic soundmark in the summer months.

Natives of the Prairies speak of the ubiquitous wind; but while I see dust in my childhood memory, I hear no wind. The Saskatchewan novelist W.O. Mitchell has written an odyssey in which the wind is the *leitmotif; Who Has Seen the Wind* is in many ways the counterpart to Chekhov's *The Steppe,* for the hero of each is a small boy.

His ears were filled with the sound of the wind, singing fierce and lost
and lonely, rising and rising again, shearing high and higher still, singing
vibrance in a void, forever and forever wild ...[2]

He found that many simple and unrelated things could cause the same feeling
to lift up and up within him till he was sure that he could not contain it. The
wind could do this to him when it washed through poplar leaves, when it set
telephone wires humming and twanging down an empty prairie road, when it
ruffled the feathers on one of Sherry's roosters standing forlorn in a bare yard,
when it carried to him the Indian smell of a burning straw stack. Once the
feeling had been caused by the sound of Gaffer Thomas's bucksaw
wheehawing impatiently on the other side of the O'Connal back fence;
another time, by a crow calling ... Always, he noted, the feeling was most
exquisite upon the prairie or when the wind blew.[3]

Other writers have remarked on the stillness of the prairie wind, the way it fills your ears and betrays no motion.

Even a hurricane is comparatively inaudible, for there are no waters to dash,
no forests to roar, no surfaces to resound, while the short grasses give forth no
perceptible rustle; and there is something awful in the titanic rush of
contending natural forces which you can feel, but cannot see or hear. The
wind may sweep away your breath on a current of sixty miles an hour, and
the clouds may rush through the sky as in a tornado, but no sounds confound
the ear. A winter blizzard, which carries on its frigid breath destruction to

2 W.O. Mitchell, *Who Has Seen the Wind* (Toronto, 1947), p.270.
3 Ibid., pp.122-23.

life, which blinds the eyes, and which drives the particles of ice and snow
with cutting force against the frozen cheek and through all but the heaviest
fur clothing, is comparatively inaudible, and the traveler appears to himself to
struggle vainly with an implacable, ghostly force which fills the whole
creation. When, also, nature is undisturbed in tranquil summer mood, and the
sky is blue and flecked with fleecy clouds floating far aloft, all sound seems to
have died out of the world, and a mantle of silence enfolds everything.
Partaking of the predominant natural sentiment, man becomes silent also; he
ceases to talk to his mates and becomes moody and taciturn.[4]

Although they moved East after they married, my parents were
both Prairie people, my mother missing the vastness of the sky and
my father maintaining the taciturnity of Prairie isolation within
him until he died. Perhaps he inherited something from the Indians,
whom he knew from encampments on the plains, and respected.
Indian eloquence has often been admired. It is unhurried and seemingly unrhetorical.

By Indian etiquette, a person speaks until he has finished saying what he
wants to. It is not polite to interrupt, and consequently to a westerner, Indian
conversations are apt to have the character of a series of short speeches. To
Indians, western practice often is impolite – as a missionary noted over a
century and a half ago: 'They are very much disgusted with the manner they
say some white people have of asking questions on questions, without
allowing them time to give a proper answer to any one of them. They, on the
contrary, never ask a second question until they have received a full answer
to the first. They say of those who do otherwise, that they seem as if they
wished to know a thing, yet cared not whether they knew it correctly.'[5]

If the environment influences behaviour, the quiet environment
of the Canadian wilderness certainly has affected Indian speech.
Canadians know it still from political broadcasts, where almost the
only voices that don't jangle and twang like used car salesmen
belong to the native people. But my father had this quiet manner of

4 C.A. Kenaston, 'The Great Plains of Canada,' in *Tales of the Canadian
  Wilderness* (Secaucus, N.J., 1985), p.4.
5 Elizabeth Tooker, *Native North American Spirituality of the Eastern
  Woodlands* (New York, 1979), p.70.

speaking and I think it was a habit with most native Canadians before urban agitations accelerated and palavered the rhythms. Though it is gradually being taken from us, isolation is a Canadian habit, inherited from a natural environment in which the voices of living nature remain mute for half a year. City Canadians don't understand this; they would have continuous commotion and chatter in the potted palm tree incubators of their neo-Florida office blocks.

'Nice place for a city,' said a Dutchman as we travelled across the Prairies on a train. The old stuffed environment of Holland still churns in his head. The little Dutchman sees nothing but an empty space waiting to receive New Amsterdam. For the rest of the world Canada is a vacant lot.

Some of these delusions of grandeur have left us interesting mausoleums with remarkable acoustics such as the marble railway stations, built during the great era of railway travel and now almost deserted. Perhaps in no other country in the world could one have the luxury of being almost the only inhabitant of a building erected for a multitude while waiting for the late night arrival of a continental train as I did in 1985 in Regina. When I arrive the station is locked, but a young man opens it for me and then goes back to his ticket counter. I cough and listen to the six-second reverberation. In the deep shadows behind the high, carved benches I think I see ghosts and hear their voices in the winter wind that pushes at the door. The steam heating clicks continuously with pinging noises. It is almost the only sound to be heard except for the wind and the muffled traffic outside, which are barely distinguishable. The young man suddenly begins to experiment with the microphone. He makes mewing sounds into it, some rather French-like words, then some letters of the alphabet and fragments of speech – scarcely anything intelligible – rather like concrete poetry. I go and speak to him. 'It will be better in the future,' he says. 'CP Air will have an office here at the station. That'll bring people back to the trains.' The telephone rings. 'Yes sir, at 7 a.m.,' he says. 'It's the Royal Hudson,' he explains, 'a steam locomotive. They bring it through every year. Lots of people phoning about it.' 'One of the greatest,' I add. 'I dunno, before my time,' he concludes. I go back and sit down. A policeman enters and knocks on one of the doors on which is written in gold lettering 'Department of Investigation.' The door opens and another police-

Monteagle Valley, Ontario. Photograph: Cheryl Bronson.

man (it could have been his double) comes out. The two of them saunter like cowboys across the tile floor, their heels clicking like bullets fired in slow motion.

The railroad figured prominently in the Canadian soundscape in its day, for the railroad was the first public machine spectacle, the first time the public saw and heard the strength of steel in motion. It also created the time zones and, with its punctual arrivals and departures, brought the clock to the countryside. The impression railroads made on the aural nerve and its significance for genetic transmission, may be deduced from the fact that children still speak of a 'choo-choo' train, though steam locomotives haven't been heard in Canada for fifty years. Another carryover is the three-toned whistle (tuned to an E-flat minor triad) still in use on Canadian railroads, respectfully honouring the three-toned whistle of the classic steam engine. At one time Canada was pockmarked with level crossings so that the long-long-short-long signal, sounded by the approach of all trains, constituted a genuine Canadian soundmark; but with the gradual removal of level crossings in built-up areas, it is only in the countryside that it can truly be appreciated today.

'They go to the Riviera and Paris, but they don't lead expeditions of discovery in their own land,' said the Group of Seven painter A.Y. Jackson. The same could be said about the Canadian soundscape, to judge by the little attention it has received to date, and even I, who have travelled and worked in many parts of the country from St. John's to Vancouver, find few notes in celebration of it in my diaries and notebooks. It was, in fact, not until I settled in Monteagle Valley in south-central Ontario in 1975 that anything like a consistent record of observations emerged. My hope to produce a recording illustrating the transformations of the soundscape in one place over a year remains unfulfilled, but I do find notes from the years after my arrival in Monteagle Valley to provide some slight notion of the annual rhythms that formed a backdrop to a decade of my work as a composer.

January 5. Early this morning I went out to collect the post. It had been very cold in the night, maybe forty degrees below zero, and from the woods all around the house I could hear the tree branches snapping, sometimes so softly the ear could scarcely trace the sound, at other times as loud as pistol shots. The sound came from everywhere around the house every two or three seconds as the morning sun rose to cast its feeble warmth on the frozen branches, expanding them.

February. The sunlight is brilliant. The evergreens are holding the snow in big armfuls. As our snowshoes sink through three to four inches of freshly fallen snow and come to rest on the crust beneath they give off a new sound: thwoom, thwoom. Yesterday on the bare crust it was thwak, thwak.

March 28. On the woodpile this evening a red squirrel singing his mating song: a single note, very fast and detached, like Morse code, his tail jumping up and down in counterpoint. From time to time one or the other of his front paws was placed on his breast, making him look like a miniature troubadour. He seemed oblivious to my presence and went on calling for four or five minutes from different perches on top of one stick of wood and then another.

April 15 and spring has suddenly arrived. It's not only the weather – a week of warm sunny weather – though undoubtedly that's the reason behind it all. It's the incredible stirring of all the living creatures in the meadows and swamps. First I noticed the frogs, faintly one evening, their high trilling scarcely audible above the breeze, for which, at first, it could easily be mistaken; but by morning it was louder, more confident. Each day since it has changed; the high shrilling began to develop a warble, then gradually it deepened, becoming more vibrant and raucous. There are still, thankfully, few insects and no mosquitoes, but there are birds. Suddenly they came in a great flood, so many varieties and colours, already pairing off and filling the air with their thrilling songs. From under a hole in the barn out poked a groundhog, standing on his hind legs to sniff the air, the wind roughing up the mouldy fur of his little red belly. But it is not only during the day that one hears the sounds of life. For several nights I've been awakened to the sounds of a furious digging near the woodshed, a tunneling that sounds hollow, almost like a mattress being repeatedly struck in an empty room. I am reminded of the old lady in Turgenev's story who hears the moles burrowing in the ground. 'That's when it's good,' she says. I was always puzzled by that statement. Now I know what she meant. The old lady is reflecting on the fact that the ground is unfrozen at last and the planting can soon begin.

April 30. The geese returned today. All day long huge flocks of them move across the sky quacking loudly as they pass north. It is a sound heard only twice a year – the last time in early October when they went south.

May 1. Frequently these days we hear partridges drumming – a deep accelerating thumping sound. It's caused by them rapidly beating their wings in the air, but sounds more like a drum. Elijah says they are blind when they drum. I've never seen one in this performance. Jean remarks that one never sees the animals of Canada; one learns about them from their voices alone. I'm not sure that I've ever seen a white-throated sparrow though they can be heard everywhere in the forest around the house. I incorporated the call into the Second String Quartet and again in the Third. Strange that the Americans know the call by the words – 'Old Sam Peabody, Peabody, Peabody' – while in Canada it remains wordless, thankfully.

May 3. By 5 a.m. it was beginning to become light and the frogs were becoming quiet, giving way to the robins' fluid singing. The sun crested at 6:15 and a few moments later flooded Monteagle Valley when a flock of about two hundred geese flew so close over the house that I could distinctly hear the flapping of their wings. The sound was like applause, appropriate to our early morning diligence in the garden – planting peas. They must have spent the night on one of the swamps nearby and were now ascending to resume their flight northward. I've heard of lost travellers finding water by listening to geese as they settle for the night – another example of 'seeing' the landscape with the ears.

May 25. Fascinating soundscape at sundown. The frogs very loud, consisting of two distinct kinds, the spring peepers with shrill voices, and their deeper partners whose name I do not know, with warbling voices. The latter were heard only to the north of the swamp. Birds mingled with the frogs – white-throated sparrows, hermit thrushes and vireos – the bobolinks were already quiet.

Then a car came along the road behind the swamp. I heard it come from the south and move slowly up the road to the north for about two miles before the hills obscured the sound. The aural illusion that resulted was striking because I couldn't confirm that the car sound originated behind the frog chorus. Of course, I know the road was behind the swamp, but I couldn't say the car was further away, based on the sensory evidence alone.

June 21. Last night about midnight I heard a howling pack of wolves. First the leader would start, then the others would join in, howling first, then ending with a kind of tense whimper. They sounded very close, certainly on my own property (an odd way to express it) and stopped as suddenly as they began. Then again this afternoon (just before I started this note) they began once more from what seemed like the same place and continued for two minutes before suddenly falling silent. Last year about this time we heard a lynx (or at least assumed it to be a lynx from descriptions of locals, who also heard it). It was a husky panting sound, like a woman sexually aroused.

A July heatwave and Elijah MacDonald arrives to help me dig holes for fence posts. 'Good fences make good neighbours,' he says. We dig without talking much while blackflies swarm around us making our faces bloody. Every time we hit a boulder he calls it a Chinaman's head and speculates on how far we'd have to go to really come out on the other side of the earth. We go on digging and sweating. He knows I'm interested in sound and occasionally volunteers a few comments on the subject. 'Old ploughshares'd make a good dinner bell, better than what you get today. Metal was tempered differently then.' Or: 'One sound I never liked is the splitting of the cow's head with the axe. You could hear it clean across the valley.'

August. A marsh hawk slowly, silently circling on the warm currents of air scarcely ever beating his wings and then so slowly that even if he'd been closer he would have remained soundless.

September 5. The sudden flight of a bird from the tall grass – the only thing to startle one on a sunny September day in Monteagle Valley.

September 27. I was lying under two trees, a poplar and a maple, and a light breeze was catching the leaves of each. But how different the sound! The maple fluttered but the poplar spun. The sound of the maple was thin and without any precise character. That of the poplar was lively, percussive and fluttery. When the whole tree was in motion it produced the impression of waves on a pebbled shore. Looking up, I noticed a distinct difference between the leaves. While the maple leaves shook from side to side on their stems, the poplar leaves were much freer, turning almost in a 180 degree arc from side to side. Combined with other leaves, the friction was therefore more considerable. In particular there were small slapping actions that added to the waves of sound – tiny percussive noises like the firing of miniature pistols. The maple leaves were larger and appeared ready to produce a richer sound (especially if one were beguiled by their more handsome colour) but in fact the opposite was the case. I have often marvelled at the sound of a bank of poplar trees in the wind (they are our richest deciduous tree aurally) but this was the first time I have observed the mechanical motion of the leaves to account for this acoustic superiority.

The deserted lake in October, after the insects and most of the birds have left. Leaves have fallen. The trees are bare. Incredibly still in the warm sunlight. No wind or water movement. The echoes of our voices across the water, long and endlessly multiplying as they hit the long line of distant hills across the lake. Go to woods. Sing to trees. Then be quiet and let the trees sing back to you.

October 30, and so warm that I can sit on the lawn and read in the afternoon. One hears only the occasional chattering of a remaining leaf or two as they rattle against the branches in the wind – so very different from the great 'breakers' of the leaves in the summer. In the distance several nuthatches and the odd jay are the only birds to be heard. A car on the newly-paved road takes two minutes to approach and then recede across the acoustic horizon. Then Neil Elliott begins a long approach on his tractor, down the hill towards me until he sounds right in front of me – though he must still be five hundred yards away – his engine pounding and only weakening when his plough scrapes a stone.

November. A large piece of cedar bark slaps against a log at the top of the barn, like a single auditor applauding the performance of the north wind.

November 28. Snow sliding off the roof in a heavy rain, layer after layer breaking off, each scraping over the roof-edge like a man clearing his throat and then dropping like balls of spit.

December 10. We just went out on the verandah. It is very cold tonight (the radio says it will go down to eighteen below) and the sky is clear. Under a canopy of stars we knocked icicles off the roof and laughed as they resounded like the notes of a glass xylophone falling and shattering noisily on the steps.

December 18. It was cold today, and tonight they are predicting that the temperature will drop to thirty-five below zero. Just now we went out on the porch. From all around the forest was crackling; erratic explosions like gunfire followed by a sizzling noise as the original detonations – caused by the branch and trunks shrinking in the cold – reverberated across the meadow. The moon was clear and the stars glistened on the snow and occasionally in the fine powdering of crystals which a telltale wind blew up. It was quiet for a while, then Jean turned and walked to the edge of the porch, her walking ferocious in the stillness, with every floorboard cracking and shuddering under footsteps. Even now as I write this by the fire, the logs of the house are making occasional snaps and thuds as the frost bites into them.

December 19. The snow was about a foot deep, covered by a crust of ice, not enough to support the snowshoe but enough to affect the sound and the touch as each foot plunged through it. Little pellets of ice scattered over the unbroken surface to each side as I plunged forward, breaking tracks to the treeline. Where the hill sloped, the ice fragments went cascading down the snow like tiny glass avalanches. I stopped to twist the branch of a bush. With a sharp snap it broke, sending little globules of ice from its twigs ricocheting in all directions with miniature soprano voices. I was profoundly aware that all the sounds I was hearing were impact sounds, sudden, scattering explosions. Then pausing at the treeline – only my

panting breath to be heard, somehow out of place in this soundscape.
Returning on the beaten trail the sound was different, the steady
explosions of shattering crystal were replaced by a fast shuffle as I
moved effortlessly over the snow I had packed down. Still I heard
four distinct sounds as I moved, for the front and back of each (meter
long) shoe can be clearly heard, the forward part of each shoe clatter-
ing in turn as the snow falls through the webbing, while the long
straight shafts at the rear sift through the snow, shrilling faintly.

Such was the annual soundscape in Monteagle Valley where I lived
and worked for nearly a decade of my life. Aside from works like
Music for Wilderness Lake, Snowforms or *The Princess of the Stars*,
I have no precise idea how living in this climate and geography
affected my work as a composer, but I know the influence has not
been unfelt. Forget where you came from and know where you are
has been my motto, and it is a good one, not only to still race consciousness, but also to assist in registering the immediacy of the
soundscape, which is always most emphatic in the present tense.

The scene shifts. We are looking out the window of István Anhalt's
home in Kingston, Ontario, at the arched doorway of the cathedral
opposite, its yellow lights glinting off the winter snow. István is talking about how he composed *La Tourangelle*, a work based on the life
of the Canadian nun, Marie de l'Incarnation, and how the scene we
are looking at inspired him. 'When we moved to Kingston from
Montreal we went back a hundred years in time,' he says. And we
continue talking about Canadian music and what inspires it, what
makes it different from that of other places. Jets from the Trenton air
base strip the sky, occasionally drowning out his voice. 'John
Beckwith's is the most obviously Canadian music,' he muses, 'not
just in its folk material, but also in its roughness. Abrupt transitions,
tedious ostinatti, broken by sudden shocks. It is like Canadian history and geography. Look at the museums. First one sees a picture of
an Indian and his family, then a picture of a logging camp in the
bush, then a picture of a Canadian Pacific Railway engine, then a
photograph of modern Montreal. There is no connection between
these things, or rather, the connections are missing except in your
imagination; events seem to pop up abruptly out of nothing. It is the

same with the space of the country. When I arrived in Halifax as an immigrant, I took the train at night and we began to make our way west. When I awoke in the morning I expected to see towns and villages. Instead I saw miles and miles, hours and hours, of trees, occasionally interrupted by sudden little clearings with a few houses clustered around a church or a gas station, then more forest. The roughness of Canadian music comes from that, and when you feel that roughness you sense that the reflection is authentic.'

I would like to think that my own music is more influenced by the country than the city, or that over the years since I deserted the city it has become more influenced in this way, but that is a matter others will have to decide. I make no apology for recording my impressions of rural rather than urban Canada in this little chronicle, for cities give me more distress than pleasure, and I think have always done so. I have long thought that every loud noise, every dissonant or jagged sound is communicating to us the suffering of the material that produced it. The crash of a window is the death rattle of glass; the squeal of tires is the scream of rubber; air shrieks pain when the jet slashes through it; metal shouts anguish inside any noisy machine.

It is an old idea. Laurentius Ventura, the sixteenth-century alchemist, wrote that when the ores of the earth 'are torn from their places, a terrible sound is heard and there follows a great fear.'[6] Pythagoras also called 'the sound caused by striking on brass the voice of a daimon enclosed in the brass.'[7] Whenever objects touch one another the sound they produce tells us quite precisely whether their contact is tender or torturous, joyful or distressing. It is an immediate and honest outburst that can never be shammed. The excessive noises of our time quite simply correspond to the accelerated butchery of the material world. Of course the countryside is not free of this, but it is in the city that it is sensed most acutely. It is a kind of music, a desperate and frightful music, mirrored in the brutality of much popular song today.

One of the more recent communication ideas is that the perceived world is not merely made up of passive material but actively selects

6 *Theatrum chemicum* (Strassbourg, 1659), vol.2, p.226.
7 Porphyry, 'The Life of Pythagoras,' in *The Pythagorean Sourcebook and Library* (Grand Rapids, Mich., 1988), p.131.

its perceivers by sending out signals to attract attention. Prior notions considered the world as a field of objects passively awaiting notice. We may take this as a switch from a visual model of perception to an aural one, for certainly sounds have never waited for us to find them – they find us. If we believe that we participate with the sensory data of the world rather than rule them, we cannot help but regard the environment with greater humility. You open to the world, waiting for it to touch you, to order you into action. Then other kingdoms of experience will begin to tell you about joys and griefs, enthusiasms and fears you had never suspected.

The verie essence and, as it were, spring-heade and origin of all musiche is the verie pleasante sounds which the trees of the forest do make when they growe.

Edgar Allan Poe quoted this line in a note to his poem *Al Aaraaf* and says he came across it in an old English tale. It would be more pleasant to believe the trees had told him, as in fact they have told countless people before and since. 'What is your favourite sound?' I once asked an Indian girl, and without hesitation she told me it was listening to the trees in the forest rub together when you put your ear to their trunks. The British Columbia painter Emily Carr called the stumps of felled trees 'the screamers,' and thought she could still hear them crying.

The mythology of Canada's native people is full of this kind of sound spiritualism. The echo of the Qu'Appelle Valley in Saskatchewan is a perfect example of an acoustic eponym, lingering at the site of a Cree legend. An Indian brave, paddling up the river, thinks he hears the voice of his beloved. 'Who calls?' he cries, 'Katapaywie sepe?' But all he hears is the wind on the water and the echo of his own voice. When he arrives at the encampment the girl has departed for the Land of the Dead Souls. And at Buffalo Lake in Alberta it is said that 'you can hear dogs barking and children playing and shouting down in the bottom of the lake. They are the ones who fell through the ice long, long ago.'[8] Enoch Baptiste, an Assiniboine Indian, tells how Lake Minnewanka in the Rocky Mountains means

8 A Sarcee Legend as told by Ella Elizabeth Clark in *Indian Legends of Canada* (Toronto, 1960), p.92.

'The verie essence and, as it were, spring-heade and origin of all musiche is the verie pleasante sounds which the trees of the forest do make when they growe.' Source: Schwarz Weiss, Paul Barz, Econ-Verlag, Wien-Düsseldorf, 1962.

'Water of the Spirits' because whenever one travelled in the neighbourhood of the lake, 'they heard the voices of spirits ... My father
heard what seemed to be the beating of a drum. The noise seemed to
be coming from the water. He could also hear voices down in the
lake.'[9]

Lake Minnewanka joins Two Jack Lake where we performed *The
Princess of the Stars* in 1985. In that work the Princess is drawn to
the bottom of the lake by an unknown force that later turns out to be
the Three-Horned Enemy. After the production, the Banff poet Jon
Whyte produced a clipping from the Banff *Crag and Canyon* telling
how in 1909 an Indian family was crossing the lake carelessly singing.

Suddenly out of the water appeared the huge back of a fish many yards broad,
only to disappear, when out shot a beautifully shaped arm and hand, which
clutched not in vain at one of the singers. Immediately a companion seized a
knife and stabbed the arm through and through. The hand only clung the
tighter to its victim and the surrounding waters were churned and lashed
about as if the winds of heaven were let loose all at once.[10]

Is this a mere coincidence or does nature hold a legacy of mysteries
into which we unconsciously tapped? Native people the world over
enriched the environment by populating it with miraculous spirits.
It was what prevented them from destroying the land needlessly.
And if deep ecology has any significance, it is an attitude we need to
recover.

Just as civilized Europeans today cannot appreciate the mysteries
of their own Eddas and Sagas, modern urban Canadians have become
equally distanced from the legends that once dignified their own
land. Still the subject is vaguely graspable by those who still live
close to nature. Who has not walked alone in a forest or meadow
without beginning to talk to the birds, animals and flowers? What
the whole world once had is still possible in the wilder parts of Canada – anywhere, in fact, away from the noises of civilization. And
behind lies the bulk of the world's mythology, or at least that produced in the northern nations and some parts of the remote south as

9 Ibid., p.97.
10 *Crag and Canyon*, Banff, Alberta, August 14-20, 1985.

well, so that it is absolutely true to assert that not only Indian and Inuit folklore makes sense here, but the Mabinogian, the Kalevala or the Eddas. In fact, all the mythology of Russia, Scandinavia, Germany or Britain can best be understood in the remoter parts of Canada, where the landscape is still uncontaminated and full of miracles.

6   THE SOUNDSCAPE DESIGNER

When Joseph Addison was writing for the *Spectator* in the early eighteenth century, he received a letter one day from a reader who had a novel idea: to regulate the sounds of the London soundscape. An unusual idea at that time, for the sounds of the city were then, even more than now, thought to be uncontrollable. Coming at a time of expansion and industrial turbulence, the heightened pitch to which the English metropolis was subjected was generally considered an affirmation of progress. This was a long time before the days of Michael Bass, who rallied the support of half the intellectuals of Britain, and managed to push into law his Metropolitan Police Act of 1864, designed to rid London of its most abusive soundswill, that of street hawkers and hucksters. That came at a time when the Empire, 'on which the sun never set,' had begun to turn its attention towards some of the shady social problems at home. It is true that writers such as Tobias Smollett had complained of noise in the streets a hundred years before this, but his were irascible outbursts rather than calls for social reform. Addison's correspondent is concerned with the same nuisance, but his solutions are more creative.

The post he desired was to be 'comptroller-general of the London Cries.' His credentials for this post were, he claimed, his 'insight into all the branches of our British trades and manufactures, and a competent skill in music.' He first divides the sounds of the streets into vocal and instrumental, the instrumental including the sounds of trades such as the 'twanging of a brass kettle or frying-pan ... the watchman's thump at midnight [and] the sowgelder's horn.' His remedy for these nuisances, unlike all later and unsuccessful attempts to cure such irritations, was not to prohibit them but to tune them. 'I would therefore propose, that no instrument of this nature should be made use of, which I have not tuned and licensed, after having carefully examined in what manner it may affect the ears of her majesty's liege subjects.'

Turning to street criers, which our correspondent considered far more offensive, he tells first of the frustrations of 'an honest splenetic gentleman of my acquaintance [who] bargained with one of them never to come into the street where he lived. But what was the effect of this contract? Why, the whole tribe of card-match-makers which frequent that quarter passed by his door the very next day, in hopes of being bought off after the same manner.' Again his cure is regulation, but regulation together with education. 'There is no just time or measure' in the street cries. He would have these matters taught. Newspapers, for instance, should be sold in 'quick time, because it is a commodity that will not keep cold. It should not, however, be cried with the same precipitation as fire. Yet this is generally the case. A bloody battle alarms the town from one end to another in an instant. Every motion of the French is published in so great a hurry, that one would think the enemy were at our gates.' What the comptroller-general would do is to ensure that some distinction be made 'between the spreading of a victory, a march, or an encampment, a Dutch, a Portugal, or a Spanish mail.' He opposes many of the most vigorous cries, considering them excessive, such as those of turnip-sellers whose wares 'are in no danger of cooling upon their hands.' And he contrasts these cries with those which are lower-keyed; for instance the cooper, who 'swells his last note in a hollow voice that is not without its harmony,' or the 'sad and solemn air' of the mender of chairs, exhorting his readers to search their own memories for other 'ditties of the same nature, in which the music is wonderfully languishing and melodious.'

If we look at pictures of city streets from the eighteenth century or earlier we note the lack of signs, particularly signs with printing. In those days all advertising was acoustic and varied with the seasons and the wares. This made for a more variable soundscape than today where the aural billboard of the shop or restaurant radio is changeless and unrelenting. The city then was still largely subject to the agrarian calendar. Recalling that the lovely song that announced dill pickling was heard for barely two months, our designer suggests that the tune might be fitted to some other words so that it should not be so quickly lost. The author senses that the basis of all soundscape design ought to be to develop the artful patterning of what is already there.

The letter concludes: 'I think it would be very proper that some men of good sense and sound judgement should preside over these cries, who should permit none to lift up their voices in our streets that have not tunable throats, and are not only able to overcome the noise of the crowd, and the rattling of coaches, but also to vend their respective merchandises in apt phrases and in the most distinct and agreeable sounds.'[1]

The letter is signed Ralph Crotchet – a musical name though, as the *Oxford English Dictionary* reminds us, a crotchet can also be 'a whimsical fancy or perverse conceit.' I suppose Addison wrote it and intended it to be taken ironically, but I detect a real concern for the quality of the urban soundscape within its paragraphs, in fact, the first real concern I have come across in any European intellectual. Mr. Crotchet wants to *study* the sounds of the street, which, at his time, were merely regarded as a swill-tub of unpleasant noises. The notion still holds, and every summer one can read letters to the editor of every urban newspaper demanding that the noise be stilled. These vigilantes of public welfare are generally intelligent enough to write vituperative and sometimes amusing letters, which are eventually followed by articles predicting that the civic officials are considering harsher penalties for noisemakers and have commissioned a new study to identify who they are, and how to kill their exuberance. 'No hawker, huckster, pedlar or petty chapman shall by his reiterated cries disturb the peace, order or tranquillity of the public,' etc. By comparison, Mr. Crotchet's article reveals a humanist with a keen interest in public education. He wants to *tune* the soundscape, not pulverize it into submission. We might say that he wants to compose the sounds of the street, not by aristocratic decree, but by giving the soundmakers something like music lessons so that their soundmaking will suffer less from cross-talk, cancellation and redundancy – in short, that it might become more harmonic.

It would seem that the World Soundscape Project, which I initiated at Simon Fraser University in 1970, was the first attempt to

---

1 Ralph Crotchet's letter can be found in 'On the Cries of London,' by Joseph Addison, in *A Book of English Essays*, ed. W.E. William (Harmondsworth, Middlesex, 1942), pp. 58-62.

take these ideas seriously. The soundscape, as I defined it then, was to be understood as the total acoustic environment, including all noises, music, natural, human and technological sounds. I wanted to study all acoustic phenomena and their evolution through history in order to determine whether there were any particular or recurrent patterns that would make it possible to determine the principles of soundscape design.

I confess that the first impulse for this study was negative. I had become alarmed by the excessive presence of noise in modern urban life. I was about thirty-five years old at the time, an age, I have observed, at which many people begin to become irritated by noise. Young people seem oblivious to it; sometimes they have an appetite for it, regarding it as synonymous with the life impulse itself. But by the time they reach their mid-thirties many people, perhaps because they have reached a level of self-confidence that inclines them to exclude the more unruly aspects of life, or perhaps merely because the tensions of mid-life make them more sensitive to irritations, begin to confess to being bothered by noise. So it was with me.

I responded by introducing a course on noise pollution in the Communications Department in which I taught. The course was not successful. What could we do but advocate better anti-noise legislation, increased protection for workers in noisy environments, more sound barriers, ear muffs and insulation – all negative measures, and feeble in a society that tended to equate increasing noise with progress.

But as I began to listen more attentively to all the sounds around me, this unsatisfying topic began to develop in a more promising way, for, as John Cage has said, 'All noises are interesting if you really listen to them.' I needed a word to describe this turbulence of pleasure and pain my ears were experiencing from the moment I awoke until long after I had closed my eyes at night. The word soundscape occurred to me. I think I invented it, deriving it from landscape, but I may have borrowed it from somewhere. It doesn't matter. I used it as a neutral word to imply all or any acoustical environments – all the sounds heard in a shopping mall for instance, or on a farm, or in an airport, or on a radio station – any environment that one might temporarily frame for study. Even a musical composition could be analysed as a sort of ideal soundscape, invented in the mind of the composer.

In a sense one could consider the whole sounding universe as a composition in which we are simultaneously the audience, the composers and the performers. The task then would be how to improve the orchestration. But just as the composer subjects himself to intensive training before writing his symphonies, we too must train ourselves before setting out to beautify the world. What are the predominant themes of the soundscape and how do they change? Do they recur or evolve? What are the balances and checks to ensure communication among all the soundmakers? What are the rhythms and counter rhythms? Is the tempo slow, fast, accelerating or decelerating? Are the sounds produced new or old, indigenous or exotic, or a proportionate blending of all kinds?

I began to set my students exercises in which they were asked to listen to and evaluate various soundscapes in this way. In the first stages these exercises are surprisingly simple. For instance:

1 / On a busy street, find the place with the quietest ambience. Where is it?
2 / Find a place where people are walking up and down stairs. Do the walkers going up make the same sound as the walkers coming down? Which are louder?
3 / Make a list of all sounds made exclusively or predominantly by men and another by women.
4 / Make an inventory of all the different sounds made by doors closing.
5 / Give me five kinds of walking surfaces producing different acoustics.
6 / Count the number of car horns (or barking dogs, or squealing brakes) you hear on a given intersection over a period of one hour.

By focusing on specific sounds I was encouraging the students to listen to all sounds. Until one begins to listen, nothing will happen. The whole body must become an ear to register with seismographic delicacy all sound sensations, the large and the small, the near and the far. The students became immediately intrigued by these exercises in sensory awareness. Now the noises of the world could be appreciated in context as a sort of percussion to an incredibly rich and subtle orchestration of perpetual surprises. Noise pollution had been flipped into a subject of positive education.

I am stressing the sensory approach as the key to soundscape studies because it is so often missed, even by the researchers themselves. Today we study sound on sonographs, oscilloscopes and sound level meters. It is a measure of how far we have got off course. The ancient Greeks, who made numerous observations of acoustic phenomena and formulated some of our basic acoustic laws, were much better listeners than today's architects and acoustical engineers. This work was initiated by Pythagorus and was extended by Euclid, Plato and Aristotle. The charm of Aristotle's encounter with listening, as recorded in his *Problemata*, is not in the answers he gives but in the ingenious questions he asks, attesting to a keen ear and empirical mind. 'Why,' he asks, 'are sounds more audible at night?'

> Why are plastered walls more resonant?
> Why are our voices deeper in winter?
> Why does salt make a noise when thrown on the fire?
> Why does cold water poured from a jug make a shriller sound than hot water poured into the same vessel?
> Why do we hear less well when we are yawning?
> Why is it easier to hear sounds from outside a house than those from inside a house outside it?
> Why is it that when one person makes a sound and a number of people make the same sound simultaneously, the sound produced does not reach correspondingly further?[2]

Aristotle expects us to test these problems first with the ear, not mathematics.

My model for developing exercises for students enrolled in my courses was that of the Basic Course developed by Johannes Itten for the Bauhaus. Itten's exercises were heuristic. They allowed for as many solutions as there were participants. But although they seemed free or chaotic, they had an incredible focus. Where Itten worked with points, lines, planes, directional contrasts, rest, motion, light and dark contrasts, I began to develop a series of what I called Ear Cleaning exercises in which the students, now better sensitized to the art of listening, worked with sounds, in fact began to create model soundscapes.

Examples of Ear Cleaning exercises would be:

2 *Problemata* in *The Works of Aristotle*, vol.VIII, bk. XI, trans. E.S. Forster (Oxford, 1927).

1 / Find a sound that makes a low thud followed by a high twitter.

2 / Try telling a well-known story without words, with sounds alone.

3 / Bring a buzzing sound to class, a tinkling sound, a thumping sound, a scraping sound ...

4 / Let four sounds inhabit a duration of two minutes.

The final exercise in my Basic Course – a sort of graduation exam – was: 'Choose one sound. Do anything you wish with it for five minutes but don't bore me.'

As this work was progressing in my courses, I began to assemble a research team to undertake some field work. I had hoped to unite acousticians, architects, urban planners, musicians and scientists involved with studying the functions of the ear, in much the same way as the Bauhaus had brought together architects, artists, craftspeople and industrialists to invent the whole new subject of industrial design. This was probably premature, but I did collect a team of talented and energetic young people, and together we embarked on our first field study: *The Vancouver Soundscape.* That

The early fire engines were provided with gongs rather than the now-familiar sirens; an example of soundscape morphology. Source: Vancouver City Archives.

work established the methodology for future research. It consisted of a book and two LP records. The book contained a resumé of the sounds of Vancouver right back to Indian times. (This was relatively easy to accomplish since Vancouver is a very new city.) We interviewed Indians, we searched public archives and we interviewed old inhabitants of the city to understand the predominant acoustic changes that had occurred over the past hundred years – a sort of soundscape morphology. We measured the prominent signals and soundmarks of the city and compared them with those of the past. We did extensive interviews with people of all ages to determine their sound preferences and their sound phobias. We documented our findings with professional-quality recordings, each of which was supported with as much historical data as possible. The document that we produced introduced Vancouver in a totally new way, and I recall the editor of a UNESCO magazine enthusiastically writing that never before had he become distantly acquainted with a city in such a vibrant and realistic manner.

No sound is heard the same way twice. The physical vibrations may not change but our attitudes towards them are always changing. That is why I consider it absolutely necessary to study the morphology of the soundscape and to conduct intensive surveys with people living in a particular environment *before* any designing of the acoustic environment begins.

Sounds that have been in a particular place for a long time I call soundmarks. Like landmarks, they define its essential character, rendering it unique. Just as there are societies for the preservation of landmarks there should be societies devoted to the preservation of soundmarks. In today's world this is more important than ever before, because landmarks and soundmarks are sensory anchors helping one to feel at home in a situation where rapid technological change can make one feel like a refugee.

Within a few years of the Vancouver soundscape study we began to receive requests for some of the sounds we had recorded, since they were no longer to be heard. Even the old foghorns were replaced by electronic instruments, higher in pitch and weaker. The fishermen said they couldn't hear them out at sea. There were letters of protest to the local newspapers but nothing could withstand the rage for progress.

While we had many musicians in our soundscape courses, I knew from the very beginning that we were not training composers but were trying to define a new profession that did not yet exist and even today does not exist to the extent desirable. I imagined a sound specialist combining technical skills and social concerns with the aesthetic sensitivity of a composer, working as an adviser, either privately or in a civic administration, to whom all matters concerning the acoustic design of future communities would be referred. Those were the skills I tried to impart to my students.

The evolving soundscape is, in fact, being designed and redesigned constantly before our ears. But whatever the motives of the designers may be, they are seldom aesthetic. The sounds produced by your telephone, your alarm clock or your computer are the results of design decisions as emphatic as any moment in a Beethoven symphony, though less inspired. From a posh magazine at hand I read of a new gadget designed for 'Powerful Personal Protection,' a 'portable alarm system that shrieks at 110 decibels to scare off attackers.'

'Noise equals power' used to be the slogan. Now it could read 'Noise equals safety,' as one listens to the stretto of car alarms, house alarms and now personal alarms, popping off around the rich and vulnerable. 'Silence equals power' is an equally valid proverb. Actually the closer one gets to individuals with enormous personal power or influence, the more one is struck by the quiet. This is as true of

The Concorde exemplifies the contradiction between visual and aural concerns in current engineering. Its sleek design makes it 'look' silent, but, in fact, it is one of the noisiest aircraft ever produced. Source: British Aircraft Corporation, 1974.

kings as it is of saints. And even today you will notice how the president of the company is shielded from unwanted interruptions: his office is high above the traffic noise; the windows are well insulated; a secretary intercepts his calls. The manufacturing of noise and the insulation from it are both examples of acoustic design. They are the extremities between which more subtle design practices must be developed. We live in an era in which practically everything we touch, see or hear was designed by humans. Some would say the world is over-designed. Personally, I can only tolerate such a world if the objects I observe and touch, or the sound objects I listen to, serve some purpose other than the accumulation of profit for their owners. It may be valid to employ music to make people work harder, faster, or buy more, but these are motives of a low order. The shaping of sound in a better world should be subject to higher values. Those that seem most appropriate are aesthetics and ecology, or rather, to be precise, aesthetics informed by ecology. Aesthetics has long been with us but ecology is new. I was thirty-five years old before I ever heard it mentioned.

The secret to ecology is finding the balance between organisms and environment. We can speak of acoustic ecology in the same way as a balancing of the sound environment. We would then be forced to reconsider the sounds and rhythms of nature – of the birds, of the wind, of the passage of seasons and the transformations of water to balance a soundscape dominated by the aggressive mechanical rhythms of today. I don't mean merely the reproduction of those sounds (though I'd rather listen to birdsong than almost any human music) but rather the study of their rhythms, durations and interplay with other sounds to solve some of the acoustic nightmares of the modern world.

A specific example: a modern railway station or airport bristles with hundreds of conflicting announcements of departures, arrivals and other miscellaneous information; yet each traveller is only concerned with one announcement; the rest is irritating cross-talk. The analogy in nature is a meadow in spring full of thousands of birds. How does each hear only what concerns it? Simple. Each species has its own distinctive call or calls. Couldn't this principle apply to the railway station? Each line would have its own identifying sound motive. Hearing it the traveller would know at once whether it was the expected announcement or not. The practice could be extended

along train or bus routes; each station stop could have its own distinctive sound cue to forewarn the passenger. Such cues would soon
become community soundmarks ingrained into the consciousness
of the traveller more unobtrusively but with greater certainty than
any verbal announcement.

If industry becomes more involved in environmental aesthetics in
the future, it will be interesting to observe how instruments such as
refrigerators, vacuum cleaners or air conditioners are handled. Can
they be redesigned without mechanical rhythms? With noise-
cancelling programs they could be rendered almost silent, but this is
not what I mean. A silent home is as artificial as a home dominated
by light industry. If we were really looking for creative solutions we
would reflect on the fact that refrigerators, vacuum cleaners and air
conditioners perform services originally provided by nature, and we
might try to endow them with sounds reflecting this fact.

This was the theme of a talk I gave in 1991 before designers from
German firms such as Siemens and BMW. I was surprised by the positive response. BMW designers would like to produce a new vehicle
with a unique soundmark so that hearing it on the street one would
turn and say 'Ah, a BMW!' Siemens' engineers are determined to
make the refrigerator sound cool so that passing it would make one
think of beer or ice cream. I recommended a mountain stream,
though their thoughts seemed inclined towards a soft high-
frequency electronic warble, alas. Still, they are thinking acoustic
design and that is new.

At the same conference Max Neuhaus spoke of his experimental
siren for future police cars, a siren beaming a more focused sound
forward, but tapered in such a way that pedestrians to the side or rear
of the vehicle would receive a less intense and more harmonic
modification of the forward sound. By 'musicalizing' the siren,
Neuhaus is attempting to humanize the police department.

One industrial noise totally in conflict with its environment is
the snowmobile. King Salmoneus tried to prove he was greater than
Jupiter by tying bronze pots to his chariot and galloping across a
metal bridge with torches blazing,[3] but for a hundred or more recre-
ationists to roar over a virgin snowfield in winter is a depravity no
pagan society would tolerate. I stopped a snowmobiler once and

3 See: Sir James Frazer, *The Golden Bough* (London, 1954), p.77.

The tranquillity of the Canadian winter is unecologically destroyed by the snowmobile; an example of negative acoustic design. Source: Information Canada Phototèque.

asked him why he wanted to wreck the winter soundscape. He objected that he had a right to enjoy the peace and quiet of nature as much as anyone – and a hundred decibels of fury stormed away across the snow. The snowmobile is considered a Canadian design triumph. Unfortunately, it acknowledges the level of soundscape design achieved to date in my native country.

Engineering decisions will become increasingly important in future soundscapes, but they are not the final word. As always, that will be determined by public attitudes. That is why I have always stressed the importance of education as the basis of all work on the soundscape. The aim is to get whole populations to listen more carefully and critically, as I believe they once did, and to learn the extent to which they can control their own acoustic environments and resist undesirable manipulations. If my own work has shifted over the years, it is away from laboratory research and the production of documents to that more necessary activity. It is preparation for the soundscape designer, who could then enter and work with the possibilities inherent in sounds already there and with the full knowledge that the value of this work was fully appreciated by the public.

MUSIC AND THE SOUNDSCAPE

In *The Tuning of the World* I predicted that by the end of the century music and the soundscape would draw together. We are nearing the end of the century; there is no need to retract what I said. I meant that the reciprocal influences between what we call music and what we refer to as environmental sound would become so complex that these hitherto distinct genera would begin to syncretize into a new art form. I was speaking of the Western world. In other parts of the world the two types have never been completely distinct, and though they now begin to show signs of separating, I wouldn't care to predict what will happen in places beyond my listening experience.

To understand the momentum for blending today it is first necessary to show how Western music differs from soundmaking elsewhere. In the Western tradition music is an abstract entertainment for the pleasure of the ears alone. The word abstract is emphatic. Listeners are not encouraged to associate music with functions or purposes beyond the aesthetic enjoyment it provides. Functional music is relegated to a lower order and music that is made to serve political, mercantile or even religious purposes is always under critical suspicion. Religious music sometimes escapes censure because so many Western composers wrote so much of it; but the conservatories and concert halls where it is taught and performed have been careful to minimize whatever religious messages it may sustain, concentrating on its aesthetic merits.

In order to achieve this purity it was necessary to separate music from the soundscape. The soundscape is a plenum. The music room is a vacuum. Music fills it. Without music in it, it is scarcely a room at all: chairs, a stage, music stands and a podium, these are its scant furnishings. But there is a method in this arrangement. All the chairs face the stage and all the sounds will come from here. This will be the exclusive focus of attention during the concert. No longer are we at the centre of the soundscape with sounds reaching us from all directions; now they reach us from one direction only, and to appreciate them we must point our ears, just as we point our eyes when we read. In this quiet space the composer will be able to fashion much more intricate structures than were possible outdoors. The music has a definite beginning and ending. The audience will arrive before the beginning and remain until after the ending, sitting in rows facing the performers. They have voluntarily surrendered the use of their bodies and their feet and will use only their hands and voices to express their appreciation at the end of the music. In order not to distract from the listening process, the performers also move as inconspicuously as possible and their faces are neutral and expressionless. Definitely the concert promises psychic rather than somatic satisfaction, and the composer uses the concentration of the audience to arrange his material in a vast architecture of principal and secondary themes, transitions, harmonic centres, modulations, instrumental interplay and dynamic shading – an ideal soundscape of the imagination, elegant, controlled, dissonance-disciplined and invigorating. The economist Jacques Attali claims to find the clue to the political economy of nineteenth-century Europe in the concert of the eighteenth century, dutifully listened to by the bourgeoisie and faithfully transmuted into a harmonious industrial order in which commodities flowed out to fill the world just as tones had filled the music hall.[1]

Sometimes I have thought the traditional sonata form is a model for a colonial empire: first theme (loud), the mother nation; second theme (softer), the supine colony; then follows the rhetorical and occasionally pugilistic exchanges of the development section, the *rapprochement* of the mother and colony in the recapitulation (both now in the home key), and the coda – consolidation of the empire. The classical music of Europe during the era of colonial expansion was a music of departures and conquests, exciting openings and exultant conclusions. That this form of music-making is unusual among world cultures is by now quite well-known. Elsewhere music is effortlessly associated with dance, with physical tasks, with religious rituals and healing ceremonies of all kinds. In those cultures

---

1 Jacques Attali, *Bruits* (Paris, 1977), pp.93ff.

there are many musics, each associated with special activities and celebrations.

In many cultures the word music does not exist at all. In Africa, for example, there is no term corresponding to music in Tiv, Yoruba, Igbo, Efik, Birom, Hausa, Idoma, Eggon or the assorted Jarawa dialects; and many other languages have qualifying terms that only partly touch our concept of music.[2] The same is true in other parts of the world: the Inuit have no generic term for music, nor can it be found in most North American Indian languages. Much of the soundmaking in these cultures might better be described as tone magic. There is a special kind of music for healing, another for bringing rain, another to ensure a successful hunt or to defeat one's enemies, etc. Even though they may all use voices and instruments, for the people in these cultures, they are not united and must never be confused. We recall also that the ancient Greeks originally employed the word *mousike* for a whole range of spiritual and intellectual activities before it gradually took on the more restricted meaning we have inherited. Ours is a special concept, nourished in the crucible of European civilization, from which it went out (along with Europeans) to many other parts of the world. What makes it special is its abstraction from daily life, its exclusivity. It has become an activity that requires silence for its proper presentation – containers of silence called music rooms. It exhibits the signs of a cult or a religion and to those outside who have not been initiated into its rituals it must appear strange and abnormal.

The thick walls of European architecture have been a shaping force behind the development of European music from Gregorian chant to serialism. In fact it would be possible to write the entire history of European music in terms of walls, showing not only how the varying resonances of its performance spaces have affected its harmonics, tempi and timbres, but also to show how its social character evolved once it was set apart from everyday life.

The great revolutions in art history are changes of context rather than style. The first big contextual change in Western music occurred when music left the outdoors and entered the cathedral; the second occurred with the appearance of the concert hall and opera house; the broadcasting and recording studio is responsible for the

2 Charles Keil, *Tiv Song* (Chicago and London, 1979), p.27.

third. Each context produced a plethora of styles but all were governed by the laws of the container in which they were generated. The music of the cathedral is unseen; it rises vapour-like to fill a large resonant space, restricting harmonic and melodic mobility to produce a hazy wash of sound blending with the mystique of Christianity's invisible God. The music of the concert hall and opera house is both seen and heard. Dryer acoustics favour faster-paced music with greater harmonic daring. It is the music of the soloist and the quick-tempered virtuoso. The broadcasting and recording studio introduced the world to schizophonia, or split sound, in which any sonic environment could, by means of loudspeakers, be substituted for any other. It pushed music into new places – in fact, any place – and prepared the way for the coalescence we are now experiencing.

The other great context for music is the original one, the outdoor environment, and this still survives as the one in which much, and perhaps most of the world's music, is produced. It is the context of street music, of the outdoor band or orchestra, of the shepherd with his Pan pipe or of women singing at the village pump. It is the context of tribal music the world over. As such, it is inclusive rather than exclusive and tends to be free rather than purchased. But above all, it blends with whatever other sounds are present. It does not seek walls for protection or an impounded audience for its appreciation.

The perception of sound can most easily be studied from the artifacts and contexts of music. This is not the only way to study the subject, but the history of music, with its cultural variants, provides a repertoire from which deductions can be made about what different eras were expected to hear, and equally what they missed, for in the study of any soundscape what is missed is just as important as what is listened to, perhaps more so. This is the 'ground' in the figure-ground relationship, and although such sounds are ignored, they are immediately noticed if they are withdrawn or if attention is directed towards them. Air-conditioning and heating systems are present in this way for modern urban listeners; so is traffic noise. (Recently, listening to a recording of music by the thirteenth-century composer Adam de la Halle, I detected the faint rumbling of traffic, anachronous to Adam's world but evidently inaudible to the recording engineers.)

The medieval schoolmen spoke of God as a presence whose centre is everywhere and circumference nowhere. It is an acoustic definition of God – as Marshall McLuhan frequently used to point out. It also conforms to listening habits conditioned by plainsong heard in the cathedral, where the singers' voices waft through the space, filling it like incense. Wherever one moves in the cathedral one is always in the middle of the sound. The concert hall, on the other hand, induced focused listening, that is, a rank-ordering of sounds in the same way that perspective painting rank-orders objects, reducing the size of the less important and moving them to the distance. Composers of the nineteenth century specialized in this dialectic of foreground, middleground and background by means of dynamic shading.

Focused listening contrasts with peripheral listening, in which the ear remains open to sounds from any direction or distance, scanning the environment for information from anywhere. It is the perceptual attitude of people who live outdoors or whose jobs involve movement from one place to another. The world is always full of sounds. They come from far and near, high and low; they are discrete and continuous, loud and soft, natural, human and techno-logical. They enter and depart in processions as events pass us or we pass by them. This is why the music of the streets has no begin-ning or end but is all middle. Something is already in progress before our arrival and it succeeds our departure. The dynamics of the sound are a product of its position in space rather than shaping by the performer.

With this in mind we might again consider how certain outdoor environments have been deliberately planned as itineraries through the soundscape. Certainly there are courtly Italian and French gar-dens laid out in such a way as to encourage the attractive passage past fountains, grottos or aviaries, and the long elegant pathways to the belvedere seem perfect for musical processions. One can scarcely visit those gardens today without imagining the festive entertainments that once glorified them. The gardens of Versailles were once the site of lavish operatic and theatrical entertainments during which the pathways and lake were illuminated by thousands of candles in silver candelabra while the fountains played through coloured lights. 'After listening to the opera or a play by Racine or Molière the king and his court would promenade until dawn or

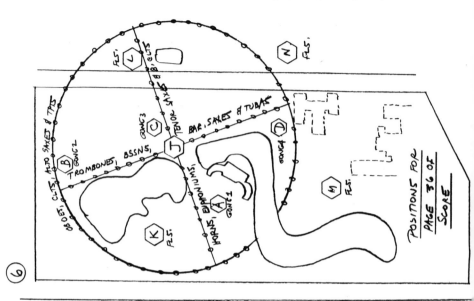

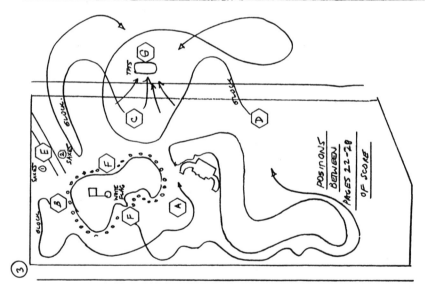

Diagrams showing the movement of musicians for the composition *Musique pour le parc Lafontaine*, Montréal, June 1992. The piece involved four brass bands moving over a wide area.

embark in flower-wreathed gondolas on the lake.'3

On the other side of the world is the seventeenth-century Kiyom-izudera (Clear Water Temple) in Kyoto, Japan. I recall walking through the ample garden with the composer Toru Takemitsu, beneath the *butai* platform where the great *gagaku* orchestras once performed. We followed the paths between the blossoms, listening to the birds and imagining how the ancient music must have sounded. Suddenly I realized how cleverly everything had been laid out to facilitate the blending of the loud and soft sounds by means of the winding path.

Years later, when I wrote *Musique pour le parc Lafontaine,* I tried to devise a routing for the musicians within this very large Montreal park that would blend both close and distant sounds for listeners no matter where they happened to be. The piece is itinerant, with the musicians constantly forming and reforming at different locations in the park, sometimes playing in processions, sometimes remaining static in geometrical formations. The work closed by passing a series of phrases from one player to the next along four branches of a cross from the centre to the periphery of the park, where another group of instrumentalists slowly moved a repeated motif in a vast circle nearly a kilometer in circumference.

When we move music from one context to another, everything changes since effects intended for one situation must be adapted to another. Listening attitudes also change. The attention of anyone in the open soundscape will constantly be flickering from one point to another; attractions of focus will be rare and unpredictable. This is what radio discovered when it deserted the living room for public spaces; program structures had to be disassembled for casual listening. Music also underwent changes: for instance, the fade-ins and the fade-outs of popular music began to simulate the effect of music passing us by, as in fact it does from the windows of open cars or store fronts.

The influences of the soundscape on music are reciprocated by musical influences on the soundscape. The diatonic tuning of car horns or train whistles are obvious examples. Right now we are witnessing the growth of synthesized tunes played from moving

3 Clement Antrobus Harris and Mary Hargrave, *The Earlier French Musicians* (London, 1916), p.21.

vehicles selling products such as ice cream (North America), propane (Brazil) or used clothes (Italy). The tunes are always well-known and often come from the classical repertoire, but almost all of them contain at least one melodic inaccuracy, due, I suppose, to the tin ear of the engineer who programmed them. In this way the 'fake' transmogrifications of well-known melodies are rendered 'real' for countless millions of people the world over so that the real tune, if ever heard again, will sound *wrong*; and engineers with no musical ability whatever become musical arrangers of incredible influence. This is how the soundscape of the modern world is being designed, failing more objective or aesthetic values.

Where the reciprocity between music and the soundscape is effectively intuited, the interaction can be like that of text and subtext, as when the rhythms of work or the motions of tools inspire the singer, or bird song inspires the flutist. Folk musicians the world over have attested to the effect of environmental sounds on their music, which is often a homage to the *paysage sonore,* as when a fiddle player was said to be able to imitate 'the squeak of a gopher ... crows calling; an anvil on a winter day ... jack rabbits bouncing off, a goshawk drifting high ... a flock of geese.'[4] And now I am thinking of a visit I made to hear an old peasant woman sing her own folksongs high in the mountains of Argentina. The audition took place in the yard of her farmhouse where we sat on tattered straight-backed chairs while the skins of freshly killed sheep dried on the clothesline, and roosters crowed in perfect unison with her singing, which consisted almost exclusively of leaps of fourths and fifths. She said the inspiration for her songs came while she made *empanadas* in her kitchen; and I don't think she realised how closely they synchronized with the sounds of her yard.

Concert music also often evoked the more populous environment beyond the music room as a kind of nostalgia. Hunting horns or spinning wheels or locomotives found representation here. In fact, the music room often assumes a kind of virtual space that is broader than its enclosure, as when soft sounds seem to fall away to the acoustic horizon or a loud sound seems to push right into the body. The frequency range of the music is another unconscious imitation of the external soundscape. Mozart's music is made up of mid- and

4 W.O. Mitchell, *Who Has Seen the Wind* (Toronto, 1947), p.189.

high-frequency sounds as was his world, whereas the heavy infrasound of the modern city is reproduced in the guitars of the modern rock group.

Composers have often been explicit about inspirations drawn from the soundscape. A couple of examples will do. Wagner describes how an alphorn invaded *Tristan:*

This act promises famously; I drew profit from it even from my Riga excursion. At four in the morning we were roused by the Boots with an Alphorn – I jumped up and saw it was raining and returned to bed to try to sleep; but the droll call went droning round my head and out of it arises a very lusty melody which the herdsman now blows to signal Isolde's ship, making a surprising merry and naive effect.[5]

George Gershwin's *Rhapsody in Blue* was inspired by a train journey:

It was on the train, with its steely rhythms, its rattlety-bang that is so often stimulating to a composer (I frequently hear music in the very heart of noise), that I suddenly heard – even saw on paper – the complete construction of the *Rhapsody* from beginning to end ... I heard it as a sort of musical kaleidoscope of America – of our vast melting-pot, of our incomparable national pep, our blues, our metropolitan madness. By the time I reached Boston, I had the definite plot of the piece, as distinguished from its actual substance.[6]

Europeans will be unfamiliar with the jazz rhythms produced by the short-section unwelded tracks of the American railroad (European rails are welded in long lengths), nor will they know how the three-tone triadic steam whistle could be warped by echoes and doppler shifts to suggest blue notes. But Walt Whitman sensed these variants when in a poem called 'To a Locomotive in Winter' he penned a line of shifting ee's: 'Thy trills of shrieks by rocks and hills returned.'

5 Letter to Minna, quoted in *The Musical Quarterly*, vol.xxxi, no. 4, October 1945, p.411.
6 Quote from the Everest Record dust jacket of *Rhapsody in Blue*, William Steinberg conducting the Pittsburgh Symphony Orchestra.

Another American composer, Morton Feldman, recalled how he gathered all the material he needed for a percussion piece *(The King of Denmark)* while sitting on a beach on Long Island.

I wrote it in a few hours, just sitting comfortably on the beach. And I can actually conjure up the memory of doing it – that kind of muffled sound of kids in the distance and transistor radios and drifts of conversation from other pockets of inhabitants on blankets, and I remember that it all came into the piece, these kinds of wisps.[7]

And this from Olivier Messiaen:

In my hours of gloom, when I am suddenly aware of my own futility ... what is left for me but to seek out the true, lost face of music, somewhere off in the forest, in the fields, in the mountains or on the seashore, among the birds.[8]

I could go on giving examples of this sort from almost every major Western composer to show that they were never indifferent to the sounds around them and frequently sought ways of incorporating these sounds into their work. It is a relatively unexplored chapter in music theory. For years I have tried to draw musicologists' attention to the fact that most of the world's music exists in counterpoise to the soundscape. Ethnomusicologists understand this but it has rarely been acknowledged by those specializing in the history of Western music. To them music is thought to be inspired by music alone: Vivaldi inspiring Bach, Bach inspiring Mozart, Mozart inspiring nearly everybody. The music schools teach of the revolutions of style: Beethoven throwing off Classicism, Debussy rejecting diatonic harmony, Schoenberg embarking on atonality. But these are mere skirmishes compared to the great contextual changes that have shaken the foundations of the art and are shaking it again today.

A few years ago the Viennese music sociologist Kurt Blaukopf began a series of studies in what he called the 'non-musical use of music.' He sensed an atrophy in the concentration habits of Western

7 'An interview with Morton Feldman,' in *Percussive Notes*, vol.21, no. 6, September 1983, pp.5-6.

8 Olivier Messiaen, *Le Guide de Concert*, 3 April 1959. Quoted from John Paynter, *Sound and Structure* (Cambridge, 1992), pp.42-43.

listeners as a result of the technical changes brought about by the new media. We all realize the extent to which music is losing its focus. It strikes us at odd times and odd places. Often two or more pieces of music can be heard in a single environment and many other sounds as well. Sometimes while shopping we hear the music of one establishment superimposed over that of another, like an over-printed photograph. Sometimes I have walked in shopping malls late at night and have overheard music playing to no one. And I have imagined a plane crash in which the only survivor will be the recorded music.

It is as if by some law of enantiodromia the Western notion of music is exploding in our faces, breaking out all around us, hemor-rhaging into new environments. Certainly the power centres in soci-ety are shifting, multiplying, so that the authority once accorded to the concert as the nodal point for musical stimulation has withered. European concert music gradually refined itself into states where even its most devoted listeners were reluctant to follow it (I mean ISCM festivals and the like); but even in its healthiest state it had given rise to a kind of aural hypertrophy in which the ear was not only isolated from the other senses but was even isolated from its more normal habits of functioning.

When I wrote the booklet *The New Soundscape* in 1968 I pro-claimed the new orchestra: anything and everything that sounds! I wanted people to begin to think of the soundscape as a macrocosmic composition in which we are all involved, and asked the question whether the orchestration could be improved. Today there are enclaves of acoustic design activity in many countries, but I have been especially intrigued by Japan's contribution, for it seems to combine fresh innovation with a traditional sensitivity to the envi-ronment. The Japanese word for music, *ongaku*, simply means the enjoyment of sounds; it is an inclusive rather than an exclusive con-cept. Thus the Tea Master may make music with his kettle.

The kettle sings well, for pieces of iron are so arranged in the bottom as to pro-duce a peculiar melody in which one may hear the echoes of a cataract muffled by clouds, of a distant sea breaking among the rocks, a rainstorm sweeping through a bamboo forest, or of the soughing of pines on some faraway hill.[9]

9 Okakura Kakuzo, *The Book of Tea* (Tokyo, 1956), p.63.

It is just such a kettle that Kawabata describes in his novel *Snow Country.*

> He could make out two pine breezes ... a near one and a far one. Just beyond the far breeze he heard faintly the tinkling of a bell. He put his ear to the kettle and listened. Far away, where the bell tinkled on, he suddenly saw Komako's feet, tripping in time with the bell.[10]

The synaesthesia suggested by aural illusions is never despised by the Japanese; on the contrary, it is cultivated. In the game known as *Ko wo kiku,* 'listening to the incense,' each scent is inhaled ceremoniously and then passed to the ear, as if somehow the resolving power of one sense was not enough to extract complete meaning, the experience being additionally complicated by the allusive name given each incense, intended to recall some scene or passage from a romance or legend.

From an active group of soundscape researchers I learned how Japanese gardeners traditionally cultivated the many variations that water produces, not only in their placement of rocks in the beds of streams to modulate the sound, but also in their use of decorative bamboo irrigation pumps (*shishiodoshi*) that tip when filled with water and drop back against stones producing pleasant hollow pitches.

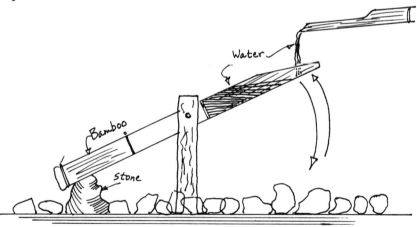

10 Yasunari Kawabata, *Snow Country* (Tokyo, 1957), p.155.

One researcher, Yu Wakao, had devoted himself to the study of water harps – resonating jars, buried under rock basins where the hands were washed before entering the tea house. The jars, which served no purpose, were set so that the spilled water that dropped into them would produce a melodic cascade of hollow pitches from below. The water harps are only found in the oldest gardens; the tradition seems to have been abandoned about two hundred years ago, but the soundscape group hopes to revive it.

These are examples of a consciousness that allows the beauty of sound to expand and permeate the whole of life; it would be futile to debate whether such things were music.

Wondering what made this thinking possible, I came to the conclusion that the traditional Japanese paper house had a good deal to do with it. One can still see such houses in Kyoto and throughout the Japanese countryside, houses with large sliding doors, carefully

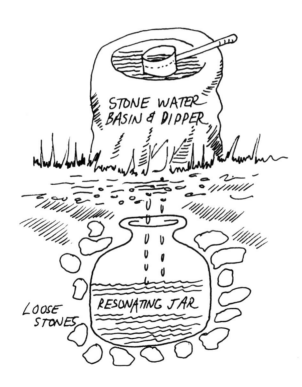

covered with rice paper. When slid back they open to beautiful enclosed gardens, the light and sounds of which reach in to fill the rudimentary and seemingly famished spaces of the house. Of course, in modern Japan (in Tokyo) such houses are seldom seen. They have been replaced by buildings of glass and concrete smudged with Muzak, for insulation from the natural environment requires cosmetics.

It seems necessary to point out that the rice-paper window is different from the glazed window. Glass resists sound; rice paper invites its penetration. Glazing is a European treatment of wall openings – the result of a primary visual consciousness; rice paper suggests aural awareness. I am reminded too that in traditional Japanese society young women were taught how to slide open such doors and windows without making unnecessary noise. Prospective mothers-in-law would test them on this refinement. The Western equivalent would be learning to crochet or managing a tea service.

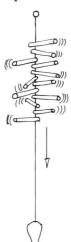

It is the absence of walls and doors that allows the Japanese, like many other people around the world, to imagine a music that may impart beauty to the environment without being self-centred or wishing to dominate the entire soundspace. The sound sculptures of Akinoti Matsumoto are typical of this unstrained attitude. A kind of *bricolage*, they are created out of simple materials to be found in any hardware shop. One of these consists of nothing more than a length of plastic fishing line with a hook at one end to attach to the ceiling and a weight at the bottom to hold it taut. Down it slither a large number of small aluminum tubes of varying lengths, drilled at one end and passed through the line. As they descend they shake, touching their neighbours to produce a delicate tintinnabulation.

Another instrument consists of a series of thin metal bars, slowly raised by a small electric motor to fall back in turn on a series of strings tuned to different frequencies. The tempo of the falling bars is very slow so that I was more reminded of the single flowers in vases one often finds in the corners of Japanese homes, or isolated calligraphy scrolls on walls, than anything approaching a music instrument.

The sound environments of Hiroshi Yoshimura have similar intentions. This is what he has to say of Sound Process Design:

What we are attempting to do, speaking generally, can be called sound design. This includes the adjustment and regulation of sound proper to an environment, along with the composition of music for environments. Possibly for a given environment just one sound would be sufficient. Sound design doesn't mean simply decorating with sound. The creation of non-sound – in other words silence – would, if possible, be wonderful in a design.

There is no question that our age, in which we are inundated with sound, is unprecedented in history. We need to develop a more caring attitude towards sounds. Presently the amount of sound and music in the environment have clearly exceeded man's capacity to assimilate them, and the audio ecosystem is beginning to fall apart. Background music, which is supposed to create atmosphere, is far too excessive. In our present condition we find that within certain areas and spaces aspects of visual design are well attended to, but sound design is completely ignored. It is necessary to treat sound and music with the same respect that we show for architecture, interior design, food, or the air we breathe.

'Wave Motion' was begun as an environment music series. This music could be said to be an 'object' or a kind of sound scenery to be listened to casually [peripherally]. Not being music which excites the listener into another world, it should drift like smoke and become part of the environment surrounding the listener's activity ... This is not music of self expression, not a 'completed work of art,' rather it is music which changes the character and meaning of space, things and people by overlapping and shifting.[11]

Yoshimura's music exists for spaces. I have heard it in galleries, where it leads nowhere but affects the space it inhabits, changing it in subtly perceptible ways. It is mostly synthesizer music, and this assists its purpose, for the synthesizer is an apparatus of all modern cultures and therefore belongs to none. Most of the background music we know is attached to known instruments and these instruments, as well as playing styles, connect it with specific periods and places: the guitar is Spanish, the accordion is Bohemian, etc. One could listen to the Muzak system in any international hotel or airport and be doused almost exclusively with American tunes played

11 From a broadsheet, Tokyo, 1983.

on vintage European instruments. This is how cultural hegemonies are secured, by subliminal advertising.

There is something to be said for the use of innocuous soundmakers in acoustic design, and there is something to be said for indigenous instruments to establish unique character. When a sound object is known and loved it functions more as a sensory anchor, assuring us that we are at home even when other features of the environment are alien or intimidating.

The soundscape designer should know these things. He belongs to no camp; he understands the requirements of the situation, adding to one and subtracting from another. He also knows the value of silence. Through his work, music, environmental sounds and silence are woven together artistically and therapeutically to bring about a new consciousness where art and life touch, merge and are lost in one another.

8 RADICAL RADIO

Radical radio. It suggests extremes. But I mean something straight from the source, for etymologically 'radical' pertains to roots or origins. And so it is by going back to its origins that I want to reconsider radio, moving from the past to the future to discover new forms of growth, immanent in the roots.

Then what was the origin of radio? Of course it is not new. It existed long before it was invented. It existed whenever there were invisible voices: in the wind, in thunder, in the dream. Listening back through history, we find that it was the original communica-

Athanasius Kircher imagined radio as a series of cones and tubes in his *Phonurgia Nova*, of 1673.

tion system by which the gods spoke to humanity. It was the means by which voices, free from the phenomenal world, communicated their thoughts and desires to awestruck mortals. The divine voice, the Ursound, infinitely powerful precisely because of its invisibility, is encountered repeatedly in ancient religions and in folklore. It is the sound of Thor, of Typhoeus, of Mercurius … to name only three of the better-known divinities who first spoke to man over the hot line. It is frequently present in the Bible: 'In the dream the angel of God called to me: "Jacob!" And I answered: I am here' (Genesis 31:11).

In those days there was nothing but religious broadcasting. The schedules were arbitrary; the programs began when least expected, in darkness, during moments of reverie or sleep, usually when alone, but sometimes before multitudes. The transmitter was always in God's hands and the power of the broadcasts was often terrifying. After he had humbled Job and reduced him to a pitiable sufferer, Yaweh raises his arm in might and proclaims:

> Have you an arm like God
> and can you thunder with a voice like his?[1]

Radio remained an awe-filled medium even after it was desacralized. There are legends that tell how the ancient kings of Mesopotamia and of China could transmit messages sealed in boxes to governors in distant provinces, who would open the boxes and hear the commands of the king. Hidden emperors are always the most frightening. To have an 'audience' with a king implies that one dares not look at him. Audience comes from the Latin *audire*, to hear. The same source provides the word 'obey' (*obaudire*), meaning to hear from below. Hearing is obeying.

That is the first thing to remember about radio. It is a fearful medium because we cannot see who or what produces the sound: an invisible excitement for the nerves, which is why I call it schizophonic (split sound) and also why McLuhan called it a 'hot' medium.

When radio was invented in the early part of this century, two models of broadcasting grew up as a consequence of this reality: the political model, born of the rage for power; and the 'enlightenment' model, born in opposition to it. The BBC, with its salt and pepper

---

1 Job 40:8-9.

diet of information and cultural affairs, exemplifies the enlightened model. Hitler gave us a vivid illustration of the other type when he wrote: 'We would never have conquered Germany without the loud-speaker.'[2] But even today, when one listens to a politician on the radio, there is a hectoring tone in his (and now also her) voice, occasioned by the enlargement of personality promised by the microphone. There may be other people on the platform or in the hall, but somehow they get only a reflex of the speech, which is clearly intended for those beyond the amplifiers.

It was significant that when, in 1916, David Sarnoff argued the case for radio in the United States, he referred to it as a modern 'music box,' thus setting in motion the idea of radio as an entertainment medium, a toy. The American broadcasting system sprang up out of fear of political tyranny. It was not to be state controlled but sponsored privately. Of course, private sponsorship eventually resulted in the tyranny of the object, as products such as soap, pop, mouth wash and sanitary pads were turned into icons that could sing, dance and fly. The first singing commercial I remember was about a banana.

I'm Chiquita the banana
and I've come to say,
bananas like to ripen
in a certain way ...

That was about 1945 and I would date the new American folklore from about that time; for unlike the printed icon, the radio counterpart achieved a voice and personality, becoming the hero or heroine of a one-minute minidrama: the commercial.

These are the theorems of broadcasting after which all modern programming is patterned. I am not interested here in a history of broadcasting. I am only interested in tracing how far modern radio

2 'I know that one is able to win people far more by the spoken than by the written word. The greatest changes in the world have never been brought about by the goose quill. The power which set sliding the great avalanches of a political and religious nature was from the beginning of time, the magic force of the spoken word.' Hitler in *Mein Kampf*, quoted by Harold Innes in *Empire and Communications* (Toronto, 1972), p.8.

has departed from radical radio in its pre-technological phase. And I will be content if you realize that considering what radio once was, all contemporary models have profaned it.

Let me build my case. When I taught in the communications department at a university, I used to give students this exercise: you are to consider yourself a visitor from another planet; your spaceship allows you to cruise close enough to pick up twenty-four hours of radio (the exercise also works for television); you are to report back to me, your commander, everything you learn about earthlings. You can imagine the result. Earthlings are obsessed with body odour. Their favourite colour is extra-white and their favourite game is trying to predict the weather. They dress in armour and move about on wheels. Their religion takes the form of a ceremony in which a sacred relic is chased about a field by opposing sects. And so forth. It is a very warped and incomplete picture, but an interesting one.

Inventories are never neutral, but to appreciate their bias one needs to get outside the society producing them. Let us become anthropologists for a moment and ask what might have happened had radio been invented by someone else. Supposing the Lendau tribe of Central Africa had invented it, would they have broadcast the rain ceremony? But this only occurred in times of drought. Or supposing the Egyptians had invented it, would they have broadcast the Osiris Festival at Abydos? But this lasted nonstop for several days. Or supposing the Bernardines of Martin Verga had invented it, would they have broadcast the singing of matins? But this took place in the middle of the night. We don't have to be anthropologists for very long to appreciate that the rhythms of other societies are quite different from our own. And at once we realize that Western broadcasting is governed and tyrannized by an instrument we have accepted as inviolable, though it belongs to no other society but ours: the clock.

Both Spengler and Mumford have spoken at length of how the clock came to regulate the destiny of the Western world. How it drove a wedge between the hours of work and the hours of leisure, timing entertainments and social affairs, regulating eating and sleeping as much as the life of the factory. Taking over the function of social timekeeper from the church bell and the factory whistle, radio became the clock of Western civilization. Throughout the day, events were shaved off to the split second. The news came at 8 on the way to work, at 5 on the way home, at 11 on the way to bed. For those on the run (or who like to think they are), there are the news and weather flashes throughout the day. Between these the tapestry of the broadcast schedule is strung. Every item has its allotted time: thirty seconds to one minute for commercials, three minutes for songs, fifteen minutes for the so-called radio 'features' – which on some stations rarely implies more than the sports report or a short interview. Full programs seldom exceed an hour, and the longest format permitted on radio is for an athletic event.

Several years ago I proposed an idea to the CBC to do a program on the sounds of the ocean. The producer wanted to know how much time I required. Without thinking I answered 'Twenty-four hours.' It seemed to me that one could not do justice to the rhythms and tides of the ocean in less time than this. I was given an hour and a half to create *Okeanos* and it was made plain how many problems would have to be overcome to make this possible. But such problems can be overcome, as the Irish Radio proved when, years later, they broadcast Joyce's *Ulysses* as a thirty-six-hour program.

Radio as we have it today is the handmaiden of the mechanical revolution, I would not say of the electric revolution, which flows with continuous currents and knows nothing of the industrial machine. Had radio been invented in 1750, factory owners would have seized it as a means of securing punctual and efficient service from their workers. No wonder employers welcome it today in banks and shops and offices as a means of improving performance in boring and stupid jobs. Today radio is the pulse of a society organized for maximum production and consumption. Of course this is temporary; radio will not keep this beat forever, or even perhaps for very much longer. The advantage of the quartz watch is that it doesn't stop or need to be reset, so the ceremonious timekeeping of radio is already anachronous. And if industrial civilization is in decline – and it is – alternative radio rhythms may be closer than we think.

The rhythms of life are enormously complex. Consider, for instance, the extended jubilation of the village wedding, the curve of the lovers' tryst, the rhythms of the sleeper, the swimmer or the long-distance runner. And from nature let us recall the rhythms of waves, of the tides, of the spinning of sand on the beach, or of the wind in Aeolian harps. Let us measure the durations of melting snow, the waning of the moon; let us again become acquainted with the counterpoint of birds and frogs and insects. Let us know these things, and when modern radio begins to buckle we will be ready to change the pulse of the Western world. You will say that such rhythms do not belong to the territory of radio; but they belong to it as much as hyperbiological rhythms do. If modern radio overstimulates, natural rhythms could help restore mental and physical well-being by putting them back in our blood. Radio may, in fact, be the best medium for accomplishing this. And when the discovery that our continued existence on this planet depends on re-establishing this continuity with all living things, I suspect that radio will reflect the discovery and play its part.

Many years ago Bruce Davis and I had an idea for what we called Wilderness Radio. The plan was to put microphones in remote locations uninhabited by humans and to broadcast whatever might be happening there: the sounds of wind and rain, the cries of birds and animals, all the uneventful events of the natural soundscape, transmitted without editing into the hearts of cities. It seemed to us that since man has been pumping his affairs out into the natural soundscape, a little natural wisdom might be a useful antidote. I still think it would be a good idea and patiently wait for its realization.[3]

The rhythms of radio are always changing, and the ingenious thinker should be aware of this. It is the rhythmic patterns that dictate content; never the other way round. At the moment, if you can put your idea into a three-minute capsule, you can move it onto radio; if you can't, you can't. This brevity shapes the treatment of all material, producing what John Leonard called the 'flat shriek' of contemporary radio.

Instead of stories, canned opinion, instead of discussion, sirens, instead of sadness, the gruesome details, instead of play, heavy breathing, fists.[4]

The limitation is not technical but cultural, for technically the radio signal is continuous and can be shaped in any way desired. Let me tell you about one rhythmic change that has begun to show up.

3 See: Bruce Davis, 'FM Radio as Observational Access to Wilderness Environments,' *Alternatives* (Perspectives on Society and Environment, Spring 1975), pp.21-27.
4 Quoted from a WQXR (New York) radio interview ca. 1981.

We all know that the average age of Western humanity is rising. I believe it was in 1971 that *Time* magazine gave the Man of the Year award to everyone under the age of twenty-one, because the mean population of North Americans was at that time under that age. Since then it has been rising. Already social scientists are aware that geriatrics is an interesting research area, and governments everywhere are promising money for programs dealing with the aged.

Now older people seek a different kind of comfort from radio than youngsters. They have their favourite programs and are less inclined to require a continuous curtain of sound to blanket their daily routines. The music they enjoy is slower and softer. The voices are older; there is less edge and frenzy to them. Then how long do you think it will be before radio rhythms begin to decelerate to please this growing and incidentally affluent public? A decade ago the CBC moved its prime evening newscast from 11 o'clock back to 10 o'clock. Why? Because older people go to bed earlier. Older people also spend less time driving about in cars. What effect will this have? Everyone knows that AM radio is designed primarily for automobile listening, that it is compressed to yield a continuous peak signal, necessary to hold it above the noise generated by the car itself, which in many models exceeds eighty decibels at higher speeds. Older people live in quieter environments; silence is more a part of their lives; they fear it less than the young. I expect these considerations to show up in revised broadcasting patterns, in the age and tempo of the announcers' voices, in the choice and dynamics of the music, in the topics of discussion, and in the methods of joining all this material together.

Listening to radio in the presence of noise (the car radio is a good example) has had a very interesting effect on programming: it eliminated it. In any noise-prone system, information has to be reduced and redundancy increased. Programs with a high information quotient (educational and cultural) are swept aside for those in which basic modules are repeated or varied slightly. The shit parade and news and weather burps are examples of such repeaters. This is not merely a matter of taste; it results more from technical considerations affecting audience environments. It certainly has nothing to do with democracy. Although Americans might cite this as the reason for low-level broadcasting in their own country, there are other countries, equally committed to democracy (Britain, Canada, France) that have had a broadcasting history emphasizing high-level intellectual programming – at least up until the time when the car radio and the shop radio and the street radio bumped it down into the Agora.

In the old days, radio programs existed as discrete entities for special interest groups. Program guides were published and consulted. I know people in Canada and Europe who would mark up the guide each week and then stay at home, instead of going out to a film, a concert or the theatre, to listen to a preferred program. Throughout my soundscape research I have tried to show how an excess of environmental noise produces sloppy listeners. We no longer listen to the radio; we overhear it. It stays on, shielding us from the coarseness of modern life. Radio has become the birdsong of the twentieth century, decorating the environment with pretty. Broadcasting as signal disappeared when the program schedule ceased to be printed. What replaced it was continuous jabberware.

Buckminster Fuller used to say that garbage was an unpackaged product. Noise is garbage. Headphone listening puts a protective seal between noise and the customer, disinfecting it. This is not a corrective in the campaign against noise pollution but a prophylactic. Nevertheless it represents a determined effort by the public to escape sonic interruptions and regain the serenity of sustained, selective listening. This too is a matter creative broadcasters should not ignore.

One of the conditions of any art form is that it must produce a metalanguage by which it can be adequately described. Poetry and painting are art forms because we have a theory of poetry and painting. This probably explains why we do not have a corresponding art form of smells; the grammar by which such an art could be analysed and criticized is too flimsy. Radio, as we have it right now, is probably not an art form, lacking an exegetical apparatus (or even an adequate program guide) for its external analysis. In *The Tuning of the World*, I called attention to the poverty of criticism dealing with this rich and potent contemporary soundscape. What we need is the study of broadcasting in terms of semiotics, semantics, rhetoric, rhythmics and form. A good radio program deserves the same critical attention as a good book or a good film. And the shapes of broadcasting ought to be as interesting to the sociologist or the anthropologist as the shape of life itself, of which they are in many ways a reflection. When I think of the number of music students who are forced to analyse Beethoven's Fifth Symphony *noch einmal*, or the number of literature students who sit down to a rehash of Keats' 'Ode on a Grecian Urn' – if only half of them were redirected towards an analysis of the radio they listened to that day, the serious criticism of broadcasting could begin, and with it, in time, the serious reforms.

You can only criticize things that happen twice. Your commentary is only valuable to others if they know they will also be able to see or hear the things you are discussing. Radio that thrives on novelty and immediacy does not encourage critical attention. But this too is a fashion. This era is intimately wedded to McLuhan's name since he was the first to catch the pulse of it. Electricity, said McLuhan, is total information. And broadcasters suddenly became aware of the all-at-onceness of the radio signal. Lawrence Blair describes it this way:

No language seems a barrier to the hidden brotherhood of 'hams' and professional radio operators. They sit, all over the world, thousands of miles apart, yet connected by electronics – the only clue to their existence being the prongs of steel emerging discreetly from their attics. This international brotherhood never sleeps, but continually monitors and feeds the thought-forms of the planet: the political upheavals, the new discoveries, the disasters, are all exchanged within moments. Teilhard de Chardin's hypothetical 'Nousphere,' an envelope of 'thought' around the world – is now quite real.

This is what we all believed twenty years ago, and I wouldn't like to estimate how many licenses were granted to broadcasters as a result of promises to bring the world to the doorsteps of larger and more remote groups of people. That was the camouflage hiding the intention to use the license to print money. The deception still thrives today. It is called 'information radio.' Its claim is to connect the listener instantly to vital events wherever they may be happening on this globe. Its aim is to maintain everything on the razor edge of the present tense. It is the special radio form of the action-packed, progressive society; and the majority of its customers are young. We have been led to suppose by its advocates (and McLuhan is certainly not innocent of this) that the potential of the medium is best realized in this way. In fact, *a* potential is realized, but when interest in it passes, information radio becomes a fashion like everything else, and fashion, as Cocteau once observed, is what goes out of fashion.

I used to have students monitor radio stations and then draw maps on which they fixed dots for every toponym in the programming – the names of towns, countries, business establishments, the location of all events, everything identified that could be tied to a place. What emerged in almost every case was a network of dots clustered around the community itself, with a vague sprinkling over the rest of the world. Looking at these maps, one couldn't avoid the conclusion that radio was intensely regionalist, mildly nationalistic and totally uninterested in the rest of the world except when it meant trouble. The whole globe may be transmitting, and satellites may be moving these transmissions around with fantastic precision, but the most healthy form of radio broadcasting today is community-intensive. It resists invasion. In fact, I doubt whether in its whole history, broadcasting (on either radio or TV) has broadened understanding for the peoples of the world to anything like the extent of the book. And despite all claims to the contrary, I don't think broadcasters ever intended to do this. Radio has been much more an instrument of nationalism than of internationalism; and when the transmitters were beamed abroad it was only for the spreading of propaganda. Commercial radio is even more tightly territorial, with networks buying up franchises as if they were grocery stores or parking lots.

Regional broadcasting seems to be gaining in importance everywhere. In countries like Britain and Germany, regional dialects, once taboo, are being actively encouraged on national programs. In Canada the CBC is dismantling its main transmission centres to make more local programming possible. These activities may be reactionary but they are certainly real. Broadcasting everywhere is beginning to give way to narrowcasting. Technical people also assure us that the 500-1600 kilohertz and 88-108 megahertz limitations will soon be overcome, making possible hundreds and finally thousands of new audio channels, fracturing the audience into a myriad of special interest groups. As these developments unfold, radio ought to become a more responsive and cybernated medium, allowing listeners to become more actively involved. In a sense, this began with the hot-line show, which is a conversion of radio back into telephony; but it must not end there. If listeners are to become a true force in reshaping radio, they must be allowed to participate in the choice of subject matter. They must not be hectored and manipulated by slick radio hosts. In Holland, for instance, Willem de Ridder operates a radio program in which any listener can make a cassette tape on a subject of his choice and it will be played on the air. The variety is astounding and refreshing.

In a similar way, I have often thought if we could just place microphones in restaurants or clubrooms or any of the places where people gather and exchange concerns, the results could be quite invigorating. A small town Kiwanis Club meeting, women at a tea party, high school students smoking behind the school house, bums on a park bench, farmers in a general store, *without* a host to keep their thoughts on target – any of these or a million other situations would yield more interesting material than opinions on the headline topics currently solicited from listeners. This too is technically possible. What prevents it is the arrogance of broadcasters.

The duty of art is to suggest alternatives to the present. In this sense all art is anti-environment. It vibrates with strange rhythms, agitating, percussing, raising, depressing, unbalancing, hurling us into new modes of perceiving, thinking and doing. Art is always detached from reality, not in time or space, but conceptually. It bends us back and sweeps us forward. Its rites and rituals are the links between the dead and the unborn, between form and possibility, between achievement and dream. Art is the enemy of the present, always wanting to change it by introducing other tenses. Art alters the perceived world by introducing new rhythms, forgotten, ignored, invisible, impossible.

What if radio became an art form? Then its content would be totally transformed. No longer would it spin as the slave to machine technology, mechanical and clocked; no longer would it palpitate with the spasms of production and consumption, singing to the rich and slobbering over the poor; it would outstrip the impedimenta of mechanization, it would drown the fury of the hawkers and hucksters, it would muzzle the voices of newscasters and news analysts. All these excrescences of the 'more' society would be shoved into the ash-bin of oblivion, and radio would begin to ring with new rhythms, the biocycles of all human life and culture, the biorhythms of all living creatures and of nature. There are people in the world today – and the history of humanity is made up almost totally of such people – who have not tried to separate themselves from nature with machines, who live organic lives within the great natural cycles of the universe, which they accept and respect. In that condition, and only in that condition, could radio be reunited with the primevally divine, charged with the energy of the sacred and restored to its original radical condition.

What I am urging is a phenomenological approach to broadcasting to replace the humanistic. Let the voice of the announcer be stilled. Let situations be presented as they occur without the interruption of sponsors, clocks or editorial manipulation. A radio station in rural Québec has the following logo:

A note of music, the song of a bird, a poet, an idea, and sometimes also silence, on the waves of CIME-FM 99.5 megahertz. You are listening to life.

Unfortunately the contents do not often live up to the claim; but it *is* approaching the theme I am announcing. Phenomenological broadcasting instead of humanistic. Reportage without the human always at the centre, twisting, exploiting and misusing the events of the world for private advantage. Let the phenomena of the world speak for themselves, in their own voices, in their own time.

I have sometimes given students the assignment of dreaming up radio programs unfettered by any restraints. Here are some of their ideas:

1 / A program about a slaughterhouse as a background to a supermarket.
2 / The life story of a giraffe from birth to death.
3 / A woman giving birth.
4 / Retarded children being fed in a nursery school.
5 / The dialogue of thieves.
6 / Place an unusual ad in a newspaper with a phone number. Record the answers.

To these, countless themes could be added. The broadcast of any ritual between animals, humans, birds or insects. If the quality of light as revealed by photoelectric eyes changes from second to second throughout the twenty-four hours of the day, why shouldn't radio register the minutest changes in the soundscape? It is the perfect instrument to do this. Why should it not be possible to record the changing of the seasons as registered in the sound of leaves, or the coming of the birds in spring? And why should it not be possible to disclose these themes with the voices of those who best understood them? The monologue of an Indian chief, complete with the deliberate and calculated silences that formed such an important part of his eloquence, and infuriated the white man. Why is it not possible for radio to take hold of the pulse of another civilization, say in the reading of Victor Hugo's *Les Misérables*, nonstop for as long as it takes? If total immersion is the way to learn languages, it's also the way to learn cultures. Or James Joyce reading the *Wake*. It's not a book anyway, it's a radio program. Or the voices of storytellers from around the world, bringing us the miraculous tonalities of the unknown; for instance, a reading of the *Thousand and One Nights*, the perfect serial, breaking, as the storyteller intended, at dawn in the middle of each episode, to continue the next night at sundown. Or programs in the middle of the night at unannounced hours – the perfect time for radio. 'Night eliminates body, day soul,' said Spengler. Or the music of Africa, and China and South America and Asia, the music of bamboo and of stones, the music of crickets and cicadas, the music of waterwheels and waterfalls, uninterrupted for hours, without beginnings or endings, just as they are in the making.

For many of these themes we will have to move out of the studio. But why not? What miserable closets broadcasting studios are – dry, cramped, antiseptic. The whole resonating world is going on continuously, and we have elected to ruminate in the latrine – which, by the way, is the only other soundproof room achieved by modern engineering. Get out into the open. Go into the streets, into the meadows, into the jungles and into the ice fields. Create from there. Flip the whole broadcasting model around and you will be amazed at what new ideas will surge within you. You will need new equipment but that will follow. Stake out the new territory and it will be designed for you – the microphone designed to record the percussion of the battlefield, to plunge into the depths of oceans or to catch the precession rates of molecules.

Twenty years ago we began to produce a series of radio programs entitled 'Soundscapes of Canada.' Our concern was to try to broaden the territory of radio by presenting the listener with unusual soundscape environments. In one program we travelled from Newfoundland to Vancouver by splicing together all the answers received

to the question 'How do we get to ...?' What the listener heard were
directions on how to get from one village or town to the next, clean
across the country, given in all the dialects and languages and with
all the idiosyncratic speaking styles of informants from every region
between east and west. Another program consisted of nothing more
nor less than three bells from a village church in Québec. Another
consisted of all the sounds of games recordists heard on their travels:
outdoor games on sandlots and hockey rinks, indoor games on bil-
liard and card tables, games with sticks and balls and words and
counters, arranged in a montage that was almost musical. We made
a twenty-four-hour recording on summer solstice in the countryside
near Vancouver, and from this extracted two minutes from each hour
to form a sort of circadian day and night. The CBC, which commissioned the series, were not very thrilled with it. They considered it
boring. They had not learned to listen, as we had, with new ears.
They had not learned that when the body and mind are prepared and
the whole being is centred, peripheral hearing replaces focused hearing, and all sounds, even the minutest, become news of the highest
interest.

It was a start. It can be built on, and radical radio is the means to
do it. Radical negation and radical affirmation. The creatively
destructive and the destructively creative. It is a Nietzschean theme,
but it is more than that. It is the theme of the living universe. Place
your microphones there and you will catch the voices of the gods.
For they are still there, Osiris in the inundation of the waters, Mercurius in the alchemist's fire, Thor and Typhoeus in the storm
clouds, and the voice of God everywhere.

9   MUSECOLOGY

For a departure take Earth Day 1990. On April 22 of that year the media sprouted green with reports of demonstrations and celebrations the world over in honour of Mother Earth. Children at school were given trees to take home and plant. In almost every major city people poured into the parks and municipal squares to discuss renewable forms of energy, natural foods, acid rain and the destruction of the world's forests – not new topics but now important to a significantly enlarged public. It was thought that a decade of ecological awareness was unfurling.

Beneath it all were silent statistics on the world's population: doubled from 2.5 billion to 5 billion between 1950 and 1987, with projections of 10 billion by 2050 according to the latest United Nations statistics. Whether nature will be able to provide resources for such numbers, and for the hopes of people everywhere for rising living standards, can be answered by no one. In the West, as if in anticipation of the expectations of people distant and unborn, conservation has become a major theme: recycling programs have been instituted by citizens and local governments, excess packaging is to be resisted, energy consumption is to be reduced.

If all things in an ecosystem are interdependent, no one, no matter what profession or occupation they pursue, can expect to remain untouched by these concerns, and this applies to musicians as equally as it does to manufacturers, politicians or children. Traditionally musicians have tried to remain aloof from social concerns, claiming that music is an abstract pursuit, a means of escaping rather than repairing the world. Taking a longer view shows that this was not always so: music has often been involved with social issues and remains deeply involved in most traditional cultures. Music may remain amoral, but its sponsors have engaged it to assist in achieving a variety of social ends, both desirable and undesirable. It may heal wounds or induce them; it may bond people together or segregate them; it has served political demagogues and commercial entrepreneurs as well as it has served holy men and rain-makers. If the issue of conservation is a serious one, music may very much become involved – and I don't mean merely by providing a rock concert in a park to end the festivities, as it did in New York, Toronto or probably a hundred other less publicized gatherings on Earth Day 1990. The question of how it may better serve these ends, or phrased differently, how these ends, if realized, may transform music, is the subject I wish to discuss.

The proponents of Earth Day 1990 prepared for circulation a list of 133 Ways to Save the Earth, which was widely reproduced in the press. They are points directed to the individual, requiring no particularly altruistic motivation to execute; they take very little time or effort, yet are sensible if one believes that healing the earth begins by cleaning up one's own space.

From this list I'm going to select a few points around which I'd like to circulate some reflections. Under 'Waste Reduction and Recycling' we read:

> Buy products that are recycled, recyclable, reliable, repairable, refillable; avoid disposables.
> Mend and repair rather than discard and replace.
> Buy products that will last.
> Avoid impulse buying.

These are all slams at the Industrial Growth Society and the unharnessed consumer spending that sustains it. The music industry as we presently have it is certainly part of this system, and its gradual commodification throughout the twentieth century has radically changed the habits of its exponents as well as its consumers. Much of this change may be attributed to the capturing and packaging of sound for profit. Before the invention of radio, the phonograph and the tape recorder, music was recycled in live performance. Musicians then devoted a lifetime to a fairly limited repertoire, which they frequently memorized. With the advent of replay systems, the repertoire suddenly expanded, neophilia broke out among music lovers and a new type of performer was required, one with an ability for quick comprehension of current techniques and an adaptability to different performance styles and playing partners. While some artists have tenaciously clung to the music they know best, many more have tried to broaden their accomplishments, often by turning to lighter or more popular fare for which their training has given them only a casual familiarity. In its worst forms this tendency has degenerated into the slippery superficiality of the studio musician and the film composer.

Long ago the critic Walter Benjamin pointed out how a work of art under the influence of mechanical reproduction begins to change: its aura begins to fade, its value as an original is undermined, the ritual of performance gives way to advertisement as the work descends to the 'universal equality of things.' More than that, new works begin intentionally to be designed for reproducibility. Once they are performed, they are, so to speak, disposable, as the artist moves on to new challenges. The result is a dynamic and changing culture, with a superabundance of artifacts, but without any real attachment to most of them. Many items have been totally decontextualized, torn from exotic roots and exhibited for their charm. African and Latin American rhythms in the service of popular and film music is a good case of this. At the moment these rhythms form a ductile accompaniment for half the entertainment industry of the Western world. Performers and arrangers are expected to master them without the slightest notion of the magic and voodoo qualities with which they were once empowered.[1] More and more music is being served up by performers who do not adequately understand the traditions relating to it or the contexts from which it is drawn.

'Buy products that will last.' No doubt when Brahms recorded his 'Lullaby' on the Edison cylinder he thought it would last. And with each generation of electroacoustic change we are offered products claimed to be permanent, the latest boast being made for the CD, which its manufacturers tell us is 'virtually indestructible.' But will it last? Unfortunately tastes change, and the biggest fashion business today is technology. The consequences for repertoire are clear: each

---

[1] A good example of a Western musician's quest to understand these powers after years of performing such borrowed rhythms is Mickey Hart's *Drumming at the Edge of Magic* (San Francisco, 1990).

generation of recording technology obsolesces all previous repertoire unless it can be transduced into the new mould. And the motivation for that is often copyright renewal. We live in an age when almost all recorded material is owned by someone. Thus we have retakes of rock and roll tunes from the 1950s and 60s as their owners try to squeeze the last buck of profit out of their properties before they fall into public domain. The record business knows nothing of originals; its ambition is 'solid gold,' a million copies rotting away somewhere.

'Mend and repair rather than discard and replace.' Musical instruments that are played continuously are generally mended and repaired, often, in the process, improving with age. They are a good example of sustainable products beside which the purchase of discs and electroacoustic appliances are mere 'impulse buying.' To arrest this impulse would signal the end of musical merchandizing as it presently exists. Art would be recycled and reused; novophilia would wane and the repertoire would stabilize.

A throwaway society will always be enchanted by the new and embarrassed by the old. This is as true of people as it is of cars. Dere-

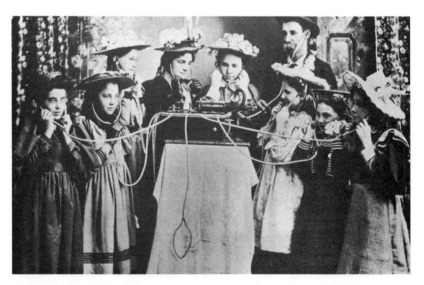

Inventions considered miraculous less than a hundred years ago are today multiplying faster than human beings and have already smothered us in waste. Source: Unesco Courier, November 1976.

liction is a mental attitude bred from faith in progress and the bur-
den of affluence. In more traditional societies, those of our own
native peoples, for instance, age does not *ipso facto* signify useless-
ness; elders retain power and cultural traditions, and artifacts are
kept intact as operative social instruments, not museum pieces. It is
in this sense that I speak of coming back to a stable repertoire, as
replacement for a hit parade driven by cash and puberty. In 1990 the
record industry generated an estimated 20 billion dollars in revenues
worldwide by providing an essentially passive consumer service.
Earth Day enthusiasts should examine their own dependence on it
and realize that the equivalent to taking a walk in the country
instead of a drive is singing your own song rather than playing someone else's.

As the Norwegian ecologist-philosopher Arne Naess points out,
any real commitment to the earth will invariably lead the individual to more active and fewer passive undertakings. When the fer-
vour for involvement does not exist, one tends to become an intran-
sigent patient, supplied with social goods and services from outside.
The extent to which we have all become dependent on electroacoustic forms of music needs wider discussion. My stockpile of
CDS is already almost one hundred and I don't even own a player.
They were all given to me by promoters. Can they be recycled?
Recycling is the first step on the road to restabilization. But consumer restraint only really begins when you stop crushing up bottles
and begin filling up the same bottle; then both the bottle and its
contents gain in value. Is there too much food in certain parts of the
world? Yes. Is there too much music in certain parts of the world?
Probably. The contraction of repertoire may be as difficult to adjust
to as the undertaking of a slimming diet, but it may one day
become a healthy necessity.

Under 'Energy' on the Earth Day list we also find some points to
consider:

> Turn down your thermostat a few degrees, especially at night and when
> the house is empty.
> Avoid air-conditioning as much as possible.
> Close off and do not heat unused rooms.
> Avoid keeping your refrigerator or freezer too cold.
> Turn down your water heater.

In vain I search the list for an indictment of the ubiquitous radio and television sets, often left dilating in unused rooms and public spaces. I suppose everyone has had the experience of wandering through a shopping mall at night or entering a restaurant at an unfrequented hour to find that one is alone with the music. Music as background sound has always existed; what has changed is that in the modern world it requires a wattage boost to achieve a hearing. Yet somehow this remains imperceptible to the enthusiasts who prepared the energy reduction list for saving the world.

There have been many indictments of electroacoustic background music in recent years, right back to the celebrated resolution of the International Music Council of UNESCO in 1969:

We denounce unanimously the intolerable infringement of individual freedom and of the right of everyone to silence, because of the abusive use, in private and public places, of recorded or broadcast music. We ask the Executive Committee of the International Music Council to initiate a study from all angles – medical, scientific and juridical – without overlooking its artistic and educational aspects, and with a view to proposing to UNESCO, and to the proper authorities everywhere, measures calculated to put an end to this abuse.

The political economist Jacques Attali realized that background music was a necessary prop to the Industrial Growth Society heralding 'the general silence of men before the spectacle of commodities.'[2] As a tool for the accomplishment of economic growth, 'music repetition confirms the presence of repetitive consumption.'[3] Attali actually goes so far as to call the modern state 'a gigantic noise-emitter, and, at the same time, a generalized eavesdropping device.'[4] The inversion of a loudspeaker into a microphone for eavesdropping, censorship, surveillance and control? Interesting idea. Certainly we know the state indulges in wiretapping; but opponents can also be tracked by means of mediatized radio phone-in shows. Music also informs the state of the moods of its citizens, for instance in the extent to which protest songs achieve popularity in times of dissen-

2 Jacques Attali, *Noise* (Minneapolis, 1985), p.112.
3 Ibid, p.111.
4 Ibid, p.7.

sion. Generally the state likes happy music and hands out licences to sponsors promising to play it. It does not like serious music or native drumming, and the music of the Middle East is considered anathema. Changes occur mysteriously. At the outbreak of the Gulf War martial music suddenly reappeared. Even hotel lobbies were flushed with victory parade soundtracks from old war movies. When the ambitions of the state and big business click together, the temperament of all music heard in public places instantly responds to such pressure changes – and I think a doctoral student or two could thump on this theme advantageously.

Musicians and music teachers have long been opponents of background music, though I have noticed that when I climb into their cars and they turn on the ignition the radio is generally on, often tuned to the local rock station. There are also cases of schools in North America where background music plays constantly, presumably because it is thought to sedate unruly students. An independent investigation of the necessity of background music in our lives is long overdue. In its present form it is relatively recent, scarcely fifty years old. As a fairly perceptive observer I have noted that banks and booksellers were the last establishments to introduce sound walls. I have also noted that the volume has risen over the years.

I have always had the impression that drugs were permitted for the same reason. From the days of the Vietnam War (the first unpopular war in history) until quite recent times, drugs have been condoned among young people throughout North America. With the critical faculties of outspoken youth anaesthetized, the Industrial Growth Society could develop its plans for global takeover unobstructed. If the crackdown on drug trafficking has begun in our time, it is only because, as the hospitals become clogged with addicts and as the rage for drugs reaches younger and younger victims, even affecting unborn children, the costs and casualties of this form of doping have begun to outweigh the benefits. The toxology of the drug business has produced a whiplash from those paying the high cost of rehabilitating the victims, and governments, once indifferent, are being forced into action.

This leaves music as the safest depressant. Its value as a means of restraining contradictory behaviour has long been known, and technological developments during the latter half of the twentieth century have made it possible to bully whole populations in this way. I recall, during a visit to the Balkans in 1959, listening to continuous folk music interlaced with political propaganda from loudspeakers on the streets of almost every town I visited. That was somewhat before the Muzak industry washed the walls of the Western world. The gradual substitution of commercial radio for wired background music is a phenomenon of the past two or three decades and it indicates a firmer determination to manipulate social behaviour, the trash of the commercials corresponding to political propaganda in controlled societies. Far from resisting the abuses of popular music, our politicians endorse it at every opportunity: Reagan hugs Michael Jackson, Jacques Chirac clutches at Madonna, Nixon gets himself photographed admiring the gold cufflinks of Elvis Presley.

The other day, in a doctor's waiting room, I was forced to listen to a commercial radio station playing disco music at an unpleasantly high volume. I asked the nurse to turn it down. Two elderly patients chimed in 'it's awful!' but the young lady refused: evidently it was desired by the staff to keep their spirits up in the basement office. I mention this as just one example of the way we are all being pushed under by music, usually chosen from an array of nearly identical radio stations by people generally young, self-serving and often ignorant, and certainly terribly nervous about silence. Strange irony: music as a displacement of silence in order to maintain silence.

Not long ago I visited a Californian university. A rock band was giving a noon-hour concert on the campus green at the imperialistic volume indispensable to this kind of music. Not a building was left unscarred; lecturers contended with the music even in the remotest classrooms, the pulsing rhythms becoming the subtext to everything that was uttered. I wandered to the edge of the campus to lose the seamy words of the songs. There I found a lonely Mexican mowing grass wearing ear muffs against the noise of the mower. As the sole beneficiary of the aural hygiene programs introduced in industry about 1970, he alone was safe.

That the Western world has been deafening itself has been well researched.[5] The term 'sociocusis' applies to deafness affecting

---

5 A few statistics: 33 percent of students entering the University of
   Tennessee in 1981 had defective hearing in the higher registers. An
   investigation at the University of Zurich showed that 70 percent of disc-
   jockeys and rock musicians examined had 'considerably reduced' hearing,

whole societies, which begins with impairment of the upper frequencies and gradually spreads downward over a lifetime, reducing the more delicate sounds of the world to muteness. Listening to loud music causes this threshold shift as fatally as any industrial noise, yet there are almost no regulations anywhere setting limits on the intensity of rock concerts or on permissible levels for headphone listening.

Why then do we assume that music is a safe drug? When states refuse to protect the health of their citizens we may assume they have another goal in mind: in this case the success of the Industrial Growth Society over the welfare of the individual or the peacefulness of the natural environment, in which, by the way, no dangerous sounds occur. Music to cover the desecration of nature. Music wired into the slums that replace it. Music to dope the youthful protester. Music to torture the independent thinker. This is the totalitarian arrangement of the modern state conjoining industrialists and politicians in their malevolent conspiracy to bring everything under their domination. Like the priests of Moloch, they cry to the musicians: 'Louder! Louder! we can still hear their screams!' And the musicians beat their brass cymbals louder and louder to cover the faint shrieks of the victims as they are dropped into the pot of fire. Noriega, flushed out of the Vatican Embassy in Panama by soldiers playing deafening rock music twenty-four hours a day – just one example of music at war.

Or are we to expect that one bright day it will occur to the U.S. Surgeon General to come out against the abusive use of music in the same way he concluded that smoking was unhealthy, thus providing the impetus for a smoke-free society? After all it is merely another form of clean air. I might expect the Earth Day proponents to appreciate this argument.

For a change of pace let's scan their resolutions on 'Food.'

Grow a garden.
Buy organic food, locally grown if possible.
Don't buy foods out of season.

---

and another Swiss investigation revealed that while 50,000 young people entering military service in 1968 showed signs of hearing loss, by the early 1980s the number had jumped to 300,000.

Organize potluck dinners.
Be creative with leftovers.

These are resolutions to bring our food consumption down and to increase its nutritional value. Tourism developed the appetite for exotic foods. I would say that cuisine is the international language today, replacing music. When I asked a class of students at an Ontario university how many had visited a Chinese restaurant, all hands went up. About 90 percent of them had visited an Indian restaurant and almost as many had been to Mexican, Vietnamese, Japanese and Middle-Eastern restaurants. None of them claimed to know much about the music of these parts of the world. Music in the modern world is a very partisan affair, carefully endorsed and censored for its propaganda value. In traditional societies, without tourism or immigration, everyone eats local food. Applied to music we might expect home-produced fare to receive a similarly upward re-evaluation, For years we have lived with a centre-margin music industry. Quality music is produced in the centres, which are often exotically far-flung cities, and is shipped to the margins, the *hinterland*, for purchase. It is a notion local groups, no matter what their skills, have been wrestling with for years.

'Don't buy out of season.' This would restore the seasonal calendar, framed by planting and harvesting. We have nothing left in our spring calendar to celebrate the planting of our gardens, and the autumn Thanksgiving dinner is merely a gobble for anyone uninvolved in harvesting.

Death and resurrection are the themes of the gardener. To coax a garden through the summer is to witness this indescribable transformation. It is like seeing your own life in miniature. The excitement of the first green shoots in the moist spring earth; vigilance against the hares and groundhogs waiting to devour them; the stronger plants spreading quickly by June, but swarming with insects of every describable colour and shape; then the long hot summer without water; you carry pail after pail as the first fruit begins to appear, never enough, until a thunderstorm breaks and the plants rocket to unbelievable heights, pushing stones aside in the triumph of their maturity; the warm autumnal days with cicadas in the trees, and you begin to start plans for storing the surplus. Your vegetables are smaller than those in the supermarket; it doesn't matter; it's the flavour; it's life and death you are eating.

Vegetation myths and rituals are central to all folklore. Osiris, Tammuz, Adonis, Attis and Dionysus personify the yearly decay and revival of life directed by the Mother Goddess. This is the theme of Sir James Frazer's *The Golden Bough*, a work showing that every society once had its vegetation rituals. Then, whole populations celebrated these mysteries together, dancing and singing in the fields. Any return to an agrarian calendar would rehabilitate the equinoxes as the pivot points for these celebrations and would attach music again to specific times and places. By extension, it would endorse all music designed for special occasions: feast days, homecomings, birthdays and weddings. Canned music would be out of place here; live music by local performers would be valued again.

The same line of thinking runs through the Earth Day 'Transportation' tips.

> Live within walking distance of your job and shopping areas.
> Bike or walk.
> Don't speed. Drive at a moderate pace.
> Avoid city driving.
> Use trains rather than airplanes; let your representatives know that you support trains.

In my days as a professor of communications, I used to set students the assignment of designing a community without cars. Of course, the community would contract: strip towns along highways would cease to exist and bedroom communities would take on full-blown life. In a sense this would be a return to what existed a hundred years ago, an era when the small town maintained control over much of its commercial and cultural life. European cities with smaller populations than Lethbridge or Brandon not only produced their Bachs and Haydns but they retained them. It was only later, with safer travel, and particularly after the introduction of railroads, that talent fled to the cities, to Paris or Vienna. In Goethe's day Weimar possessed a thrifty population of five thousand, yet it held on to some of Germany's greatest poets and became a centre of pilgrimage for many of its best intellectuals and artists, including Beethoven. North American towns and villages resonated with their own indigenous culture in those days too: every town had a band, some had orchestras, most produced locally-written plays, and a few tried their hand at creating operas. My grandmother sang in a village choir in Warsaw, Ontario (population ca. two hundred); the choir practised three nights a week and occasionally toured. Today these towns and villages are cultural slums, margins fed from external centres, or at best, conduits through which road shows occasionally pass. An energy crisis could change all this.

When one reads the writings of the anarchists William Godwin or Peter Kropotkin, one realizes that what they were really arguing for was regional integrity against the controls of the megastate. The preservation of independence was to be maintained without 'obedience to any authority, but by free agreements concluded between the various groups, territorial and professional, freely constituted for the sake of production and consumption as also for the infinite variety of needs and aspirations of the civilized being.'[6] A pluralistic society, thus constituted, would resist the authority of any interest group growing in power to a point where it could bully smaller groups into submission. With the growth of regionalism we are witnessing an instinctive attempt to accomplish just that. To assist creatively in the restoration of life on a smaller scale, musicians would have to renounce a lot of their imitative tactics and find their inspiration elsewhere than among the superstars of the industry, as is the case now. They would have to turn to the ethnic groups of their own areas and ultimately to the environment of their own regions.

Under the Earth Day heading 'Preservation of Life and Environment' one item attracts my attention as being of potential significance for musicians:

Avoid buying wood from tropical rain forests.

This is a criticism of what is happening in Brazil ... or Canada. I want you to understand the role music has played in helping to define the ambitions of the megastate as opposed to the self-contained community, and to do this we must look at the physical materials from which musical instruments are made. The powerful

6 Peter Kropotkin, quoted in *The Essential Writings of Anarchism*, ed. Marshall S. Schatz (New York, 1971), pp.xi f.

and imperialistic megastate looks outward for its resources; the self-contained community looks inward.

Consider a native Indian who has made a drum from an animal he has killed. The animal was his totem, his ancestor. Whenever he plays the drum the animal continues to speak. Its voice is united with his voice, and, whether conscious or unconscious, this bonding can never be absent from his song. It was Marius Schneider who suggested that every traditional musical instrument involved the sacrifice of a living being in its construction – a haunting idea.

Consider a shepherd who has made a flute from the reeds of a stream. There is a perfect commentary on this in the opening of Rumi's *Masnavi*, called 'The Lament of the Reed Flute.'

> Hearken to the reed flute, how it complains,
> Lamenting its banishment from its home:
> 'Ever since they tore me from my osier bed,
> My plaintive notes have moved men and women to tears.
> I burst my breast, striving to give vent to sighs,
> And to express the pangs of my yearning for my home.
> He who abides far away from his home
> Is ever longing for the day he shall return.
> My wailing is heard in every throng,
> In concert with them that rejoice and them that weep.
> Each interprets my notes in harmony with his own feelings,
> But not one fathoms the secrets of my heart.'[7]

That the material of a musical instrument may have a home other than its carrying case, or that it might inwardly be longing to return to its native element, is a notion that never occurs to a Western musician today. Or if it did, it would be embarrassing, since many of the materials, like the wood of the Brazilian rain forest, are the products of plundering: gold, silver, ebony, ivory, the rosewood of xylophones, the granadilla of oboes. These aren't materials from your backyard; they come mostly from Africa, Asia and South America, and were originally taken by colonial powers to Europe, where they were fashioned into instruments, trophies, you might say, of the plundering. When the citizens at home listened to the swelling

7 *Teachings of Rumi*, trans. E.H. Whinfield (New York, 1975), p.1.

chords of the symphony and saw all that glitz on the stage, they were ostentatiously reminded of their glorious empire 'on which the sun never set.' And the music swept out in crescendo after crescendo in fulfillment of this prodigious dream of flourishing colonies and prosperity at home. Some of the materials may have changed but the subtext to music marketing today is identical.

An ecologically responsive music would reduce its dependence on foreign materials as much as foreign inspiration, and seek both closer to home. And by materials I also include electricity, the prime material of the electrified band. The anarchists would have sought to introduce a diversity of energy sources to prevent concentrations of power. I watch with amazement as the whole music industry plugs in to the same energy source, often dangerously produced or extracted from someone else's territory, and wonder when this realization will occur to them. In *Music in the Cold* (1976) I wrote: 'Art within the constraints of a system is political action in favour of that system, regardless of the content.' Electrified music supports environmentally reckless projects like that at James Bay no matter what your tastes.

In the spring of 1990 I was in Brittany during a terrible wind storm that put the electricity out for a day. Even Paris was blacked out for three hours. There was no news, no telecommunication from the nerve centre of France, and it struck me how easy it would be to take over a country by detonating its power house. Telephone calls were reduced because the computerized Minitel directory didn't function. You couldn't phone a doctor or a hospital because you couldn't find the number. Locally there were some interesting changes: cash registers couldn't be opened and shopkeepers began calculating with pencils; postage meters refused to dispense stamps; there was no bread in the village because the baker had his dough in a large, electrically-operated kneading machine and the dough couldn't be removed. Music, of course, was also deadened by the blackout. Perhaps it is only in a state of emergency like this that one realizes the extent to which music today, no longer under the control of the breath and fingertips of the performer, runs the risk of falling into total oblivion faster than any other musical tradition the world has ever known.

It is time to sum up. The Earth Day list ends with a few points under 'Philosophy.'

Use simple means in your daily tasks and avoid unnecessarily
    complicated instruments.
Avoid 'novophilia' – love of what is new merely because it is new.
Appreciate ethnic and cultural differences among people.
Cultivate life in your community.
Celebrate seasonal changes, solstices and equinoxes with special
    observances.
Reduce stress in your life.
Do physical work.
Have fun and be joyful.

To accomplish the goals of the Earth Day enthusiasts the present
day music industry would have to be restructured. For one thing, the
relationship between the passive consumer and the active performer
would call for modification. Community-oriented performer-
teachers would be required in greater numbers, and audiences would
have to cease regarding themselves as mere customers of entertainments engineered for their benefit. The recording industry would
have to collapse.

We would then be reduced to the status of a developing nation.
But developing how? Developing by the re-investiture of music-
making for all. 'No one sings a wrong note in our tribe,' an Indian
once said to me. This doesn't mean there are no virtuosos, no singing
masters in Indian society. It merely means that everyone has a place
in the community of singers.

Dolores LaChapelle, a follower of Indian ways and an interpreter
of what has come to be known as 'deep ecology,' that is, a belief in
the equality of all forms of life in their diversity, interaction and
symbiosis, has written that 'rage and destruction at all age levels –
small child, teenager and adults come from being left out of "the
story."'[8] Then how do we put them back into the story? The
ecologically-aware musician of the next millennium may give some
thought to this.

8 Dolores LaChapelle, *Sacred Land, Sacred Sex, Rapture of the Deep*
   (Silverton, Colorado, 1988), p.133.

10 I HAVE NEVER SEEN A SOUND

Now I wish to speak of sounds.

The world is full of sounds.

I cannot speak of them all.

I shall speak of sounds that matter.

To speak of sounds, I make sounds.

I create – an original act which I performed the moment I emerged on this earth.

Creation is blind. Creation is soundful.

'In the beginning God created the heaven and earth' – with his mouth.

God named the universe, thinking aloud.

The Egyptian gods came into being when Atum, the creator, named them.

Mithra came into being out of vowels and consonants.

The terrible gods came into being out of thunder.

The fruitful gods came into being out of water.

The magic gods came into being out of laughter.

The mystic gods came into being out of distant echoes.

All creation is original. Every sound is new.

No sound can be repeated exactly. Not even your own name. Every time it is pronounced it will be different. And a sound heard once is not the same as a sound heard twice, nor is a sound heard before the same as a sound heard after.

Every sound commits suicide and never returns. Musicians know this. No musical phrase can be repeated exactly the same way twice.

Sounds cannot be known the way sights can be known. Seeing is analytical and reflective. It places things side by side and compares them (scenes, slides, diagrams, figures ...). This is why Aristotle preferred sight as 'the principal source of knowledge.'

Sights are knowable. Sights are nouns.

Sounding is active and generative. Sounds are verbs. Like all creation, sound is incomparable. Thus there can be no science of sound, only sensations ... intuitions ... mysteries ...

In the Western world, and for some time, the eye has been the referent for all sensory experience. Visual metaphors and scaling systems have dominated. Interesting fictions have been invented for weighing or measuring sounds: alphabets, music scripts, sonograms. But everybody knows you can't weigh a whisper or count the voices in a choir or measure a child's laughter.

It is probably going too far to say that in aural culture, science, especially physics and mathematics and their dependents – statistics, physiology, empirical psychology, drafting, demography, banking, etc. – the list is long – would disappear. It is probably enough to say that in purely aural cultures they don't appear.

Have I got off the track?

I was saying that everything in the world was created by sound and analysed by vision. God spoke first, and saw that it was good second.

What happens if it isn't good? Then God destroys with sound. Noise kills. War. The Flood. The Apocalypse.

Noise cancels. It turns language into a polyglot; the case at Babel. When the noise of the world became so great that it disturbed 'even the inner parts of the gods,' they released the Flood (*Epic of Gilgamesh*).

Some say the noise of the apocalypse will be of ear-splitting intensity (Mohammed in the *Qur'an* or John of Patmos in Revelation). Others maintain 'the world will not end with a bang but a whimper.' In any case, it will sound, because all traumatic events maintain sound as their expressive medium: war, violence, love, madness. Disease alone is silent and yields to analysis.

Come with me now and sit in the grandstand of life. The seats are free and the entertainment is continuous.

The world orchestra is always playing; we hear it inside and outside, from near and far.

There is no silence for the living.

We have no earlids.

We are condemned to listen.

I hear with my little ear ...

Most of the sounds I hear are attached to things. I use sounds as clues to identify these things. When they are hidden, sounds will reveal them. I hear through the forest, around the corner, over the hill.

Sound gets to places where sight cannot.

Sound plunges below the surface.

Sound penetrates to the heart of things.

When I disregard the things to which sounds are attached, the phenomenal world disappears. I become blind. I am swept away sensuously by the vast music of the universe.

Everything in this world has its sound – even silent objects. We get to know silent objects by striking them. The ice is thin, the box is empty, the wall is hollow.

Here is a paradox: two things touch but only one sound is produced. A ball hits a wall, a drumstick strikes a drum, a bow scrapes a string. Two objects: one sound.

Another case of 1 plus 1 equals 1.

Nor is it possible to join sounds without them changing character. Zeno's paradox: 'If a bushel of corn turned out upon the floor makes a noise, each grain and each part of each grain must make a noise likewise, but, in fact, it is not so.'

In acoustics, sums equal differences.

Sounds tell me about spaces, whether small or large, narrow or broad, indoor or outdoor. Echoes and reverberation inform me about surfaces and obstructions. With practice I can begin to hear 'acoustic shadows,' just like the blind.

Auditory space is very different from visual space. We are always at the edge of visual space, looking in with the eye. But we are always at the centre of auditory space, listening out with the ear.

Thus, visual awareness is not the same as aural awareness. Visual awareness faces forward. Aural awareness is centred.

I am always at the heart of the sounding universe.

With its many tongues it speaks to me.

With the tongues of gods it speaks to me.

You cannot control or shape the acoustic universe. Rather the reverse. This is why aural societies are considered unprogressive; they don't see straight ahead.

If I wish to order the world I must become 'visionary.'
Then I close my ears and create fences, property lines, straight roads, walls.

All the major themes of science and mathematics as developed in the Western world are silent (the space-time continuum of relativity, the atomic structure of matter, the wave-corpuscular theory of light) and the instruments developed for their study, the telescope and the microscope, the equation, the graph, and above all, number, are silent likewise.

Statistics deals with a world of quantities that is presumed to be silent.

Philosophy deals with a phenomenal world that is presumed to be silent.

Economics deals with a material world that is assumed to be silent.

Even religion deals with a God who has become silent.

Western music is also conceived out of silence. For two thousand years it has been maturing behind walls.

Walls drove a wedge between music and the soundscape. The two fell apart and became independent.

Music within; pandemonium (i.e., devilry) without.

But everything that is ignored returns. The vehement obscurity of the soundscape pushes back to confront us as noise pollution.

As an articulated problem, noise belongs exclusively to Western societies. It is the discord between visual and acoustic space. Acoustic space remains askew because it can't be owned. It becomes disenfranchised – a sonic sewer. Today we view the world without listening to it, from behind glassed-in buildings.

In an aural society all sounds matter, even when they are only casually overheard.

'At the time when you hear the cry of the crane begin the winter planting' (Hesiod: *Works and Days*).

In Ontario, the signal to stop tapping the maple trees is when the spring frogs are heard; then the ice has melted, the sap is darker, the syrup inferior.

Another example: a man walks across the snow. You know the temperature from the sound of his footsteps. This is a different way of perceiving the environment; one in which the sensorium is undivided; one which recognizes that all information is interconnected.

Some sounds are so unique that once heard they will never be forgotten: a wolf's howl, a loon's call, a steam locomotive, a machine gun.

In an aural society sounds like this can be brought forward and mimicked in song and speech as easily as a visual society can draw a picture or a map.

The visual society is always amazed at the aural retentiveness of people who have not yet passed through the visual phase. The *Qur'an*, the *Kalevala* and the *Iliad* were once memorized.

Remember that.

Visual man has instruments to help retain visual memories (paintings, books, photographs). What is the device for retaining aural memories?

Repetition.

Repetition is the memory medium for sound.

Repetition is the means by which sounds are retained and explained.

Repetition is the means by which the history of the world is affirmed.

Repetition never analyses; it merely insists.

Repetition makes the listener participate in the statement not by comprehending it but by knowing it.

'It is written, but I say unto you ...' And I will say it again and again and again, because Hearing is Believing.

As the grip of the visual-analytical world weakens and is replaced by intuition and sensation, we will begin to discover again the true tuning of the world and the exquisite harmony of all its voices.

We will find the centre.

Then the whole body will become an ear and all sounds will come to you, the known and the unknown, the sweet, the sad and the urgent.

When my body lies white and blue in bed at night, then all sounds come to me of their own accord, unhurried, strangely blended, the light-toned and the slow grinding of mountains. Then hearing is most alert ... and there is singing before me ... as I pass beyond 'to the land that loveth silence.'